In 1994 *From Strength to Strength* won the inaugural Australian Book of the Year Award. The sequel, *The Strength in Us All*, has continued the success of the first, and along with *Outback Wisdom* and *Some of My Friends Have Tails* they have firmly established their place as Australian classics, becoming four of the best-selling Australian books ever.

Combined sales of Sara's books have now reached almost one million copies and they continue to feature in best-seller lists.

Sara lives at Bullo River with her daughter Marlee, Marlee's husband Franz and their little boy Ben. As well as managing the property, she is in constant demand as a motivational speaker, is well-known for her work in the campaign against breast cancer and, in her 'spare time', writes books.

To Mum,

Hope you enjoy this,
Happy Reading!

all our love
Jane, Gary & Jackson
xxx

5.98.

Also by Sara Henderson

From Strength to Strength

From Strength to Strength (audio tape)

The Strength in Us All

Some of My Friends Have Tails

Outback Wisdom

SARA HENDERSON

A Year at Bullo

Sun
Pan Macmillan Australia

First published 1997 in Macmillan hardback by Pan Macmillan Australia Pty Limited.
First published 1998 in Sun by Pan Macmillan Australia Pty Limited.
St Martins Tower, 31 Market St, Sydney

National Library of Australia
cataloguing-in-publication data:

Henderson, Sara, 1936–.
A year at Bullo : around Sara's table
ISBN 0 7251 0759 6.
1. Cookery, Australian. 2. Northern Territory –
Social life and customs. I. Title.
641.5994

Food styling: Janice Baker
Photography: Peter Johnson
Design: Kathie Baxter Smith
Recipe consultant: Anne Marshall
Thanks to: R.M. Williams, City Store.
Palomino Riding School, Belrose.
Shack, Mosman. Royal Doulton.

Printed in Australia by McPherson's Printing Group

Dedicated to the great cooks in my life:
Mary, Marlee, my sister Sue and my sister-in-law Frances,
and in memory of my darling Mum and Mary.

Contents

Introduction

ell, here I am just starting to write the introduction to *A Year at Bullo* but the rest of the book has already been edited! I always do the introduction last because once I start writing a book it seems to take on a life of its own. I just pick up a pencil and follow.

I receive so many requests from people wanting to know what it is like to live on a station in the middle of the outback. What do we do? What do we eat? How is our life different to people who live in the city? Since I can't take you all to the station I've tried to bring the station to you. And the best way of doing this is to take you through *A Year at Bullo*, month by month.

A life on the land is a life dictated by the seasons. The work that we do and the food that we eat is all dependent on the weather. I especially wanted to write about food as it is such an important and vital aspect of our lives at Bullo River. On a remote working cattle station we need to constantly refuel the bodies of working men and women and there is certainly no takeaway or home delivery! If we don't cook it ourselves, we don't eat it. And after thirty years of cooking three meals a day for over twenty men I think I can safely speak with authority on the subject of food.

As you read *A Year at Bullo* I hope that you will start thinking about food in a different way. Instead of letting your eyes and nose do the thinking (and leading you to the nearest takeaway) let your brain direct you to fresh food prepared by you in your own kitchen. Even if you are not working on a cattle station, food is still a very important part of your life. It is what sustains you and keeps you alive. It can make you well or it can make you ill. It is important to understand exactly what you are eating and where it came from, to make time to enjoy and digest your food.

At Bullo River meals are a social occasion, a time to sit down together and reflect and relax. Out in the outback change comes slowly, so some of the wonderful old routines of days gone by are still in practice on the land. Meal times on the station still hold great significance and our working day revolves around them.

I grew up in a different Australia to the Australia of today. The population was three million, not seventeen million, and fresh food was a normal part of life. I can remember going to the butcher, greengrocer and fruit shop daily. We took our own containers for tea, sugar, flour, etc and carried it home in a string bag. Groceries were ordered weekly from a reliable firm by the name of Moran & Cato. A strange little sober man, dressed in a bowler hat, white shirt, black tie, trousers, highly-polished shoes and a calico apron would seriously write down the order and tip his hat in farewell. The order would be delivered in impeccable condition.

The baker delivered fresh bread in a cart every day. The cart was pulled by a horse who would walk to the next house and wait while bread was being delivered to the previous house. Fresh milk and eggs also came by horse-drawn wagon. Meals were a time for the whole family to get together and talk.

Of course it is impossible to go back to those times and that's not what I'm suggesting that we do. But there are many benefits in following the example of the past. Food in season is fresher and cheaper. If you cook yourself you know exactly what you are eating and it gives you a feeling of achievement. Food cooked at home is usually healthier than takeaway. Cooking and eating in our own homes also forces us to spend time with friends and family. It brings us together and allows time for talk. Taking our own packaging to the supermarket cuts down on waste and helps solve our environmental problems. There are just so many benefits – socially, health-wise, economically and even environmental – in preparing food at home. And as some of the stories in this book reveal, food can also be a great source of laughter and it can even bring strangers together.

Even though *A Year At Bullo* goes through the twelve months of a year, it is not just one year of my life, but rather events, stories and memories drawn from many years and brought together to make for you an interesting read. I hope that you get a few good laughs out of these new stories, enjoy the recipes and think seriously about food in a new light.

January

Steamed Crayfish/Rock Lobster or Crab

❧

Fresh Herb Sauce

❧

Orange Lemon Lime Sauce

❧

Mango and Basil Sauce

❧

Pan-Fried Tasmanian Salmon

❧

Quick Fresh Mango

❧

Mango Sauce

❧

Our Favourite Green Salad

❧

Garlic Croutons and Bacon Pieces

❧

Summer Anchovy Dressing

❧

Winter Sour Cream Dressing

❧

Health Drinks

❧

Fruit Smoothies

❧

Lemon and Raisin Slice

❧

The station wagon manoeuvred slowly along the rough track, easing carefully into each unavoidable pot hole and climbing steadily out. I had one eye constantly on the precious cargo, one eye on the dirt track ahead.

The full moon bathed the valley in a silver-white haze. Headlights weren't necessary at the speed I was travelling, with the moon being as bright as an overcast twilight, but they did highlight the extra-deep holes I needed to avoid. The beams continued to wind, searching through the wilderness, startling cows and their calves grazing in the cool of the night as well as the occasional flock of emus or wallaby in flight.

Three kilometres down the valley the headlights picked up the first of the ploughed fields, fields that continued way beyond their beam. I switched off the lights and waited in the moonlight. In the distance I could see the tractor lights randomly tracing patterns on the landscape and then across the evening sky, illuminating great swathes of stars as the big machines turned or went up and down an incline in the large paddock.

Marlee and Franz were planting our hay crop for the next dry season, working in the north-east corner of the paddock. I slowly skirted the field in that direction and after a kilometre or so I started down a slight incline into the lower part of the paddock, the noise of the engines finally coming up to meet me. My headlights picked up the outline of the maintenance trailer and the Toyota, both parked on the edge of the ploughed field. I looked at my watch: 11.45 pm.

'Good,' I thought. 'Plenty of time to set everything out and attract their attention.'

Opposite: Sara in front of the bull catcher with her dogs. Left to right, Jet Jet's nose, Munro and Sumie. Following pages: Lunch by the billabong. Steamed Lobster with Mango and Basil Sauce (recipes pages 14–15) and Our Favourite Green Salad (recipe page 24).

It was New Year's Eve, and Marlee and Franz were working through the night, rushing to plant our hay crop before the approaching storm brought the rain. If the storm continued on its present path it would be perfect timing – we would finish the planting just before the rain. If, however, the rain beat us, the paddock would be too wet to finish the seeding and with the follow-up rains coming in fast, the tractors would not get back into the paddock for the rest of the rainy season. Then we would only have half the hay we needed.

I looked once more to the north-east horizon. Lightning played a constant, silent staccato rhythm on the moonlit sky. The approaching storm held all the promise of being spectacular.

No sound of thunder came to me on the still night, only the constant drone of the tractors at the bottom of the paddock. The storm was at least sixty kilometres away but how fast it was travelling was anyone's guess. The tractor lights flashed up into the sky. They had just turned the north-east corner and were coming up the paddock towards me.

Marlee and Franz had been ploughing and planting for a week now. Our crops grow during the rainy season and are harvested in the dry when the rain's over, but planting is a constant gamble. We must wait for the first heavy storms of the season before we till, because the ground at the end of the dry has not seen rain for six to seven months. If we plough before the rain, the high winds will blow away all the top soil.

So we wait until after about ten centimetres of rain soaks the soil – enough moisture for us to get the ground ready for seeding. The seeding has to be done in between the storms, and before the ground gets too wet to work. Every year it is a constant lottery to see if we can get the crop in before the rain arrives.

When the rains are late, and the monsoonal trough finally descends and covers northern Australia, we find ourselves working through the night in between low depression downpours or the storms that herald their coming with massive displays of sheet lightning and deafening, bone-shaking thunder.

This was one of those wets.

Opposite: The bounty of Bullo. Roast Beef (recipe page 153) with baked vegetables, Baked Chinese Barra in Foil (recipe page 99), Pavlova with Marlee's Special Filling (recipe page 236) and assorted salads.

The ploughing was finished after the first heavy rain and we had been working around the clock to get the seeding done before the mass of lows and cyclonic depressions descended on us for the rest of the rainy season.

It just happened to be New Year's Eve and not many more hours before the storm reached us, effectively finishing tractor work in the paddocks for the season.

Marlee and Franz had been working all day, since four in the morning. They'd stopped for a quick lunch, come in at dinner – grabbing a quick snack along with a few hours' sleep – and then they'd gone straight back to work, shouting to me over their shoulders, 'See you next year!'

I sat for a while staring at the distant hills, before deciding I did not want to spend this night alone. I headed for the kitchen, to prepare a New Year's Eve midnight feast. We'd dine in the field, under the full moon. A surprise!

The picnic table was set with plates, glasses, cutlery, candles, a few silk roses in a vase and a bottle of French champagne in a bucket of ice.

The eskies contained lobster, our favourite green salad with summer dressing and crunchy French bread loaves still warm from the oven, light-ly spread with a herb butter. Because of the heat, the food stayed in the eskies until the very last moment.

I had made an easy, but tasty and cooling dessert to follow the lobster: fresh mangoes, kept in the freezer until almost frozen, served cold with mango sauce and topped with some whipped cream that actually survived the journey! I excelled myself by making a 'naughty but nice' slice to go with the chilled coffee and finished the meal with some homemade orange peel dipped in chocolate.

As the lights finally turned the last corner heading towards me I flashed the station wagon lights to signal I was there and watched as the tractors slowly approached.

They were a good way through the field – about one third done. It would be a close call if they finished before the storm hit. The tractors stopped, falling silent almost as soon as they saw my signal. The two dark silhouettes walking quickly across the field became larger and larger until finally Marlee and Franz stood before me.

'I thought you might like a midnight snack, seeing it's New Year's Eve, and a glass of champagne to celebrate.'

'Great, I'm starved. Let's eat!' exclaimed Marlee. Franz just nodded, popped the cork and poured the champagne.

We clinked our glasses, took a good gulp, sighed, and said, 'Here's to a great year!'

I glanced at my watch and saw that it was a few seconds past midnight. 'Happy New Year!' we all shouted in unison as we gave each other a kiss.

As well as enjoying the good food and company, it was wonderful to just sit in that vast field, the ploughed earth disappearing over the horizon into the darkness, the machines silent in the background, looking like monsters ready to pounce. I looked around and saw that the entire valley was bathed in the unusual light only a full moon can create. In the beautiful magic of this setting we talked about the plans we had for the coming year and what we hoped to achieve. We wondered just what the year would bring, hoped that we could handle it and ate with gusto!

The eskies were empty in a very short period of time. As we sat contentedly sipping our coffee, the faint rumblings of thunder warning us not to dally too long.

'There's the back-to-work signal,' said Franz. They both stood, stretched and gave me a kiss. I handed them each a thermos flask of coffee and a couple of rounds of sandwiches to see them through the night.

'See you for breakfast,' I called, as they once again became dark shadows against the moonlit sky, hurrying towards the machines.

I sat a while enjoying the memories of the meal. The roar of the engines became a distant drone as they moved away to the far end of the paddock.

It had been a lovely New Year's Eve, the dinner just right and the three of us together in that truly unique setting. Marlee had to admit she was impressed, since I hadn't cooked for years. I, too, was slightly amazed at my efforts. I lost the desire to cook long ago after far too many years of cooking for twenty or more, three times a day, seven days a week. But I felt that this particular night needed a special effort, so I managed to motivate myself.

I gathered up the remains of our meal, packed everything into the station wagon and started back home. When I reached the gate the two sets of tractor lights were heading up the field towards me. I flashed a goodbye and watched as two sets of eyes blinked back at me in the night.

I looked at the endless freshly ploughed earth, bathed in moonlight, the approaching storm lighting the heavens in a continuous display of chain lightning, the two sets of tractor lights slowly circling the vast field, intent on the job at hand, and I had to admit that it had been a great New Year's Eve. I don't suppose that there are many people in the entire world who have had a New Year's Eve quite like that.

As I approached the homestead, the dogs barked furiously at the approaching headlights. They raced out to challenge the intruder – prepared to defend the house to their death – only to squirm and wriggle with delight at my return.

There was very little food to put away. It seems when we are excited about plans for the future, or talk enthusiastically about our hopes and dreams, we eat faster! I washed the dishes, cleaned the kitchen and left the washed eskies open to air. In December and January the weather is so humid that a closed esky can develop mould within twenty-four hours.

After such a wonderful meal I didn't feel like sleeping, so the dogs and I sat, contemplating the heavens and the year to come. My thoughts went back over the night – it was always the spontaneous events in our lives that are the most memorable.

I also thought about the way that certain emotions become so firmly connected with memories of food. I will never again be able to eat any of those dishes without thinking of that night – the field, the moonlight and the company would instantly return to my mind just at the mention of that food.

However, it did seem strange to be sitting in a ploughed field in the middle of outback Australia eating lobster. What were we doing eating lobster? Well, the lobsters – a whole carton of them – were a gift from some very nice fishermen who spent time fishing at Bullo.

They mentioned they were lobster fishermen from down south and asked if we would like some fresh lobster sent by air freight when they arrived back home. What a question! Of course, we said 'Yes!' and they did ... they sent the lobsters. It was quite a campaign – an enormous amount of coordination went into the journey of the lobsters, from down south to Darwin.

They had to time the departure day with one of the days I was returning to the station so the lobsters could go straight home with me from Darwin. But some of the best-made plans can go wrong and this one did.

I went to the air freight department to pick up the carton. After reading the contents of the box the man in the office offered to take it off my hands, 'if it was a bother'. I thanked him and said I thought I could manage.

Then the plane was delayed by weather, so I booked into a hotel overnight. I asked if the lobsters could be put in the kitchen chiller. The clerk said he would stick a very large red sign on the top of the carton to ensure that the lobsters were not used for dinner. He also offered to help me by relieving me of my burden! Well, the chef didn't serve the lobster to anyone for dinner and eventually the box and I boarded the plane and headed for Bullo.

Imagine my surprise when I finally got home, opened the carton and found the lobsters still alive! I backed away in horror as the memories came flooding back … memories of thirty years ago in the kitchen in Maryland when I lifted the plastic garbage lid and saw all those squirming, angry crabs!

'Oh no, they're alive!' I screamed.

'Don't worry, Mum. I'll take care of them,' said Marlee. She smiled at my discomfort, remembering my sheer hysteria from all those years ago, even though she was only a young girl at the time.

I left the kitchen at high speed and Marlee did what was necessary without me knowing anything about what followed, which was just the way I liked it. Since the 'crab affair' I have never, ever tried to cook anything 'alive' ever again. Whenever I go near a lobster or crab, it is always cooked and ready to eat.

However, if you want to cook lobster, or crab, this is what I was taught in crab country, Chesapeake Bay, Maryland, and way up in Maine, America's lobster country. The methods of cooking are almost the identical.

You always steam lobster and crabs. It is sacrilege to cook a lobster in water, according to the northern experts.

Steamed Crayfish / Rock Lobster or Crab

1 uncooked crayfish / rock lobster or crab

1 teaspoon celery salt

1 teaspoon mustard powder

1 teaspoon chopped fresh parsley

1 teaspoon paprika

1 teaspoon salt

8 grinds freshly ground black pepper

1 cup flat beer

Firstly, take a large deep saucepan or boiler (there are special, fish-steamer pots with a rack inside them but they are expensive and, let's face it, we do not cook crayfish or crab every week). If you can't find a wire rack to fit in the saucepan, use a colander turned upside-down. The aim is to elevate the crayfish or crab above the water.

Fill the saucepan with water to a level 3 cm below the rack or the top of the upturned colander. Cover and bring to the boil. Meanwhile, in a small bowl, combine celery salt, mustard, parsley, paprika, salt, pepper and beer. Stir well.

Put the crayfish or crab onto the rack; cover quickly with the lid (or you could end up in my position, with an angry crayfish or crab racing around your kitchen floor)!

After a few minutes, when the poor thing has expired, you can pour the beer mixture over the lobster to add flavour while cooking. Adjust heat so that liquid is bubbling gently.

Make sure the lid is tightly sealed; steam crayfish/crab about 20 minutes per kilo. It will turn an attractive red-orange colour when cooked through.

You can eat it warm with many delicious sauces and some of my favourites follow. Or eat it cold with fresh lemon juice, freshly ground pepper, sea salt and a sprinkling of coarsely chopped fresh parsley.

SERVES 2 – 4, DEPENDING ON SIZE OF SHELLFISH

Fresh Herb Sauce

4 teaspoons / 20 g butter

2 spring onions / shallots

3 teaspoons chopped fresh thyme

2 tablespoons Drambuie

1 cup cream

1 teaspoon cornflour

Melt 3 teaspoons butter in a heavy-based saucepan over a medium heat. Add spring onions and thyme, gently fry until onions are soft, about 1 minute.

Stir in Drambuie and cream. Bring almost to the boil; reduce heat to medium–low and simmer for a further 1 minute. Mix cornflour and the remaining table-spoon of butter to a smooth paste. Add gradually to mixture in pan, stirring constantly until mixture thickens.

Serve sauce with freshly cooked warm crayfish and sprinkle with a mixture of chopped fresh herbs.

SERVES 4

Mango and Basil Sauce

1 large or 2 small mangoes

2 tablespoons fresh lemon juice

1 tablespoon fresh lime juice

½ cup fresh basil leaves, loosely packed

¼ cup olive oil

Peel mangoes, remove stone. Place mango flesh in a food processor or blender. Add lemon juice, lime juice and basil. Mix until smooth. Slowly add oil with processor or blender still in operation. Continue to add all the oil until sauce is smooth. Serve chilled with cold crayfish or crab.

SERVES 4

Orange Lemon Lime Sauce

2 teaspoons finely grated
orange rind

2 teaspoons finely grated
lemon rind

½ cup fresh orange juice

½ cup fresh lemon juice

½ cup fresh lime juice

1 tablespoon finely chopped
spring onions/shallots

2 cloves garlic, crushed

2 teaspoons reduced-salt
soy sauce

1 tablespoon grated ginger

1 teaspoon chopped fresh
parsley

1 tablespoon cornflour

Combine orange rind, lemon rind, orange, lemon
and lime juices, spring onions, garlic, soy sauce, ginger and parsley in a heavy-based saucepan. Bring to
boil over a medium heat. Reduce heat and simmer
for 5 minutes, stirring frequently. Blend cornflour
smoothly with 1 teaspoon water. Add to saucepan
and bring to the boil, stirring, until sauce thickens.
Serve with freshly cooked warm crayfish or crab.

SERVES 4

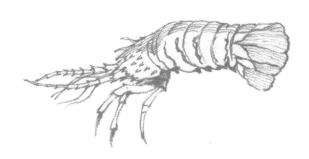

Another food from our New Year's Eve feast that has many memories for me is French champagne. Everyone has a story or memories that go with a bottle of French champagne, but the story that always pops into my mind of late has to be that of the very shy young man – at least he seemed shy to me in the split second that I did see him.

I was signing books at a bookstore in Adelaide when a package appeared on the table beside me. I looked up to see a young man escaping out of the store, very intent on not being seen or stopped. I looked inside the paper bag to find a bottle of champagne, two punnets of strawberries and a card.

The card said he had read *From Strength to Strength* and especially liked the part where Charlie kept me from shopping in Hong Kong by feeding me champagne and strawberries for breakfast. He hoped I could maybe have a breakfast the next morning of champagne and strawberries, in memory of Charlie.

Little did he realise that just about ten million things reminded me of Charlie, but he certainly did hit one of the popular chords with the champagne and strawberries. And yes, I did think of Charlie at the start of the new year, sitting in the field sipping champagne, as I often do when I do anything, every day of my life.

I smiled at the stars as I relived the memories and the dogs and I walked sleepily towards the bedroom.

I woke early to the sound of heavy rain on the roof. I don't think there is any other sound that can compare to heavy rain on a tin roof. It has such a wealth of indications in the north. It assures you the crops will grow, that there will be hay for your animals. It gives relief from the relentless heat and settles the dust. It gives you a clear view of the mountains, their images distorted by heat waves for past months. It brings overcast skies, cool cover from the sun's rays, and green grass for the animals after months of dry. It lulls you to sleep at night and wakes you first thing in the morning.

Rain in the north is a guarantee that life can continue for another year at least.

The dogs greeted me enthusiastically and it was a full five minutes before I could switch on the water jug in peace. When there are three of us in the house, it is not too bad. But with just one person, you really have your hands full, coping with a bunch of very active, affectionate dogs who are determined to inform you they are pleased to see you. They will not be denied the morning greeting ceremony or their toast and Vegemite.

I glanced out the French doors and saw that the Toyota was missing. Franz and Marlee were not back from planting. They couldn't still be working – the rain was too heavy. It looked like the forward edge of the storm had arrived and the worst was yet to come. They would have seen this as well and would have ensured that they were out of the lower paddock before it was too late.

I looked down the road, towards the field; nothing – just black low clouds and torrential rain. No movement on the ground. I started to cook breakfast, hoping they would arrive soon. I put the finished breakfast in the oven to keep warm and waited for the sound of the Toyota coming up the flat.

It never came.

When someone is overdue, I immediately start thinking of all the things that could have gone wrong. On the land the list is endless. I started through the list. If one of them was hurt, the other could manage to get them home. The possibility of them both being hurt was very unlikely.

They were bogged, I decided. That had to be the reason for the delay. The heavy rain would put the lower paddock out quickly. I decided to drive to the end of Nutwood paddock, because it was halfway and it was unlikely that I would get bogged there.

I headed for the bedroom, closely followed by the dogs, and changed into my jeans, good heavy walking shoes, a hat and a raincoat. As I headed for the door, two drenched, bedraggled figures appeared outside. Soaked to the skin and squelching with each step, Marlee and Franz waddled inside, their hair plastered flat on their faces.

'Hi, Mum, what's to eat? We're starved!' said Marlee in a cheerful voice, followed by, 'Wow, is it cold!'

They took a quick shower, put on dry clothes and we all sat down to a hearty breakfast. They were both extremely chirpy for two people who had worked all night and then walked several kilometres in the rain.

'We finished the seeding about fifteen minutes after the rain started. As you can imagine, it was getting pretty sticky out there in the paddock.

'I got the Toyota and trailer to high ground and Franz moved the big tractor out, but bogged it halfway to high ground. The second tractor bogged just outside of the paddock gate and the Toyota is bogged at the bottom of Nutwood. So we walked home. We can dig them all out when the rain stops and everything dries out a bit.

'But ... we got the crop in! Happy New Year, Mum!'

They went to bed and slept until lunch.

January usually finds me writing. By the time we get through Christmas, New Year and planting the crops, I often don't start until early January. Depending on the rain each year, it could be as late as mid-January.

January, February and early March are my heavy writing months. All cattle work stops around October or sometimes as late as November, if the weather is kind. Most of the staff leave in November and December, depending on what work projects are being finished that year.

So January finds us down to just the family and the dogs. It rains endlessly and the grass grows overnight; you mow it whenever it stops raining. If the rain doesn't take a break the grass just encloses you after four or five days. Even 12,000 head of cattle, 300 horses and all the wildlife cannot make an impression on the grass in January and February – if only the feed would last all year!

We spend weeks on end guarding the sorghum crops from the thousands of cockatoos that cover the skies in flocks over a kilometre wide. We wouldn't mind so much if they were truly hungry and needed to eat. But the cockatoos just walk along the rows and dig out all the seeds. And it is not because of hunger – it is just a game to pass the time. Franz approached a bird sitting in the field that didn't move at all. Franz thought it was dead until he was just a metre away and it started thrashing around on the ground, squawking. It couldn't fly because it had eaten so much seed! When the seeds that the birds haven't eaten manage to become plants, they walk along the rows of new plants, pull them out and then leave them on the ground to die.

Left undisturbed, the cockatoos can destroy a whole paddock of crops.

The Ord River farmers seem to have the answer, as Marlee found out when she called the helicopter company to hire a chopper to do some work with our cattle. The reply was, 'Sorry, we're all on "cockatoo" patrol.'

The farmers hire choppers for the few hours at dawn and dusk – the cockatoo feeding times – to fly back and forth over their fields, stopping the cockatoos from landing to eat the seeds and the baby plants. This is quite successful for the farmers, but unfortunate for us. We are just over the hill from the Ord River farms and so the cockatoos flee from the helicopters and come over the hill to drive us up the wall!

This time of the year is seriously hot in the northern outback. Life-threateningly hot, in fact, if you are in the wrong place at the wrong time. That can be something as simple as just being broken down on the front drive, with a thirty kilometre walk ahead of you, back to the homestead.

The heat makes us thirsty all the time. Working outside is only possible in the early morning and late afternoon. You have to drink an average of two litres per hour throughout the day or you can suffer dehydration. So when the temperature reaches the mid-forties, as it does in January, we have a problem keeping up with our water intake. In fact it is close to impossible to consume what we need, if we are in the sun and moving. We never ever step outside the homestead without a large water container – it becomes part of us. And I am not talking a small hip flask, we are talking eight-litre containers.

It has been calculated that you can't carry, comfortably, enough water for a day's walk – if you were stupid enough to try to walk all day in the heat of the wet season.

So water, as you can see, is an important part of our diet. The standard eight glasses a day does not apply in the north in the hot months – we drink that in the first few hours of the day.

We find that we want to eat anything icy or cool. A grilled steak with salad is usually welcome after sunset. When the heat of the day subsides, the mind and stomach turn to thoughts of solid food. Opposite is a lovely light recipe that we often eat on those hot January nights.

Pan-Fried Tasmanian Salmon

You will need:

1 salmon fillet per person, 180g to 200g each

Brush a very thick, heavy-based frying pan with olive oil. Heat pan over a medium-high heat; add salmon and seal both sides of the fillets, until they have a golden brown appearance, turning once, about 2 minutes on each side.

Transfer salmon to a shallow baking dish and bake in a moderately hot oven/190°C, for 12 minutes or until cooked.

In my opinion, this is the only way to cook any fish, but lots of people like things a little more fancy. So if you want more out of your salmon, before cooking you can marinate 4 salmon fillets in a mixture of:

¼ cup olive oil
8 sprigs fresh mint, chopped
1 clove garlic, crushed
1 teaspoon light or reduced-salt soy sauce
freshly ground rock salt to taste
freshly ground black pepper to taste

Place the fish fillets on a sheet of foil; pour the marinade mixture over; wrap up and marinate in the refrigerator for 15 to 20 minutes.

Remove fish from foil and pan-fry in a heavy-based pan, then bake for 12 minutes, as recipe directs above. Serve with salad or freshly cooked vegetables and rice.

SERVES 4

In the wet season, sunset also brings the bugs! And any light attracts them in the thousands, so we have to eat either just before sunset or in the dark to have any peace. Bugs just kamikaze into our food. Most of the bugs you can see, but stink bugs are tricky and if you accidentally chew one, you never eat after dark again!

The longing for cold food continues throughout the wet season. So we find a long line of cold meals and cold desserts become our regular favourites: ice-cream with tasty sauces, mousse, smoothies – anything, as long as it is cold or icy.

During January I often freeze milk, with some vanilla and grated nutmeg stirred in before freezing. It takes a long time to eat with a spoon, is satisfying because it is so cold, good for you because it is high in calcium, and because it takes so long to get through, it is good for the waistline as well!

One of my all-time favourite cold desserts is Quick Fresh Mango with Mango Sauce. It is the dessert we had for our New Year's Eve midnight feast and the recipe follows.

Quick Fresh Mango

6 mangoes, peeled, stoned and sliced

¼ cup caster sugar

⅓ cup rum

vanilla ice-cream, whipped cream and Mango Sauce (see following recipe) for serving

Arrange mango slices in a shallow dish and sprinkle with sugar and rum. Cover and chill in the refrigerator for 1 hour or so.

Serve the chilled mangoes in individual dessert dishes spooned over ice-cream; pour Mango Sauce over; top with whipped cream and sprinkle with praline if desired. (If you are trying to be good, diet-wise, just serve the mangoes with the sauce. For our 'feast in the field' we had to leave the ice-cream back home in the freezer and be content with the Mango Sauce and whipped cream. Ice-cream melts in a few minutes in the wet season at Bullo.)

Serves 6

Mango Sauce

2 mangoes, peeled and stoned

2 egg yolks

¾ cup caster sugar

1 tablespoon cornflour

½ cup milk

2 tablespoons passionfruit pulp

In a blender or food processor mix mango flesh until smooth. Beat egg yolks, sugar and cornflour in a small bowl until thick and creamy.

Heat milk in small saucepan; slowly add egg yolk mixture, mango puree and passionfruit, stirring constantly. Stir over a medium heat until mixture boils and thickens. Cool. If sauce is too thick, thin with a little cream or orange juice.

You might find after you have the following salad a few times, your taste for it will increase. By the end of a week at Bullo 'non-salad eaters' are eating as much as we do.

Our summer dressing has all the good things we need in the constant heat of the northern summer. Do not put it over the salad; serve it separately and let each person help themselves. This enables the salad to keep for an extra day or so, in the fridge with a damp towel over the bowl. And the salad does not turn out oily. But there is nothing like a fresh salad so it is better to work out your requirements and make just enough. You will find it will always be eaten, no matter how you keep increasing it.

Our Favourite Green Salad

1 large lettuce or as many varieties of mixed lettuce leaves or salad greens as you like to equal 1 large lettuce

2 cups coarsely chopped fresh parsley

2 cups thinly sliced spring onions/shallots

½ cup snipped fresh chives

250 g parmesan cheese, finely grated

1 cup garlic croutons

½ cup cooked bacon pieces

½ cup Summer Anchovy Dressing (recipe page 26)

or

1 cup Winter Sour Cream Dressing (recipe page 26)

Wash and dry lettuce leaves. Wrap in a clean tea towel and crisp in refrigerator while preparing remaining ingredients.

Tear lettuce leaves into a large salad bowl. Add parsley, spring onions/shallots, chives, cheese, croutons and bacon pieces.

Sprinkle dressing over and toss gently until evenly coated and combined. Serve salad immediately.

SERVES 8 – 12

Opposite: Quick Fresh Mango with Mango Sauce (recipes page 23).

Garlic Croutons and Bacon Pieces

10 cloves garlic, crushed

½ cup olive oil

10 thick slices day-old or stale bread

½ cup chopped parsley

8 rashers bacon

To make Croutons: Crush garlic cloves into a wok or a large heavy-based frying pan. Add oil and heat gently on a medium–low heat until the flavour of the garlic infuses (goes through) the oil, about 5 minutes.

Lightly toast the bread; cut into small 1 cm squares; add to the garlic oil; toss gently and cook until the croutons are crunchy. Drain the croutons on paper towels to remove as much oil as possible. Mix croutons with parsley. Cool, then add to salad.

Store the extra croutons in a sealed glass jar in the refrigerator for future salads or to sprinkle over soups. If they go soft, just spread out on a baking tray and bake in a moderate oven/180°C, until crunchy again.

To make Bacon Pieces: Remove bacon rind and bones, using kitchen scissors. Cut into very small pieces (about 1 cm square) and cook in a preheated heavy-based frying pan over a medium heat until very crunchy. Drain on paper towels and cool, then add to salad.

Store extra cooked bacon pieces in a covered container in the refrigerator, for future salads.

Opposite: Pan-Fried Tasmanian Salmon (recipe page 21).

Summer Anchovy Dressing

1 x 45 g can anchovy fillets,
well drained

1 tablespoon wholegrain or
Dijon mustard

6 large cloves garlic, crushed

¼ cup chopped fresh parsley

¼ cup snipped fresh chives

½ teaspoon freshly ground
black pepper, or to taste

1 x 375 ml bottle
(1½ cups) red wine
vinegar

¾ x 750 ml bottle
(2¼ cups) extra virgin
olive oil

Place anchovies in a mixing bowl; mash or pound to a paste. Add mustard, garlic, parsley, chives, pepper and vinegar. Mix well.

Slowly drizzle oil into anchovy mixture, whisking constantly with a wire-balloon whisk, to form a well-mixed emulsion. The dressing will separate on standing so whisk well just before use.

Store extra dressing in a non-metal screw-top jar in the refrigerator and shake well before using.

Winter Sour Cream Dressing

½ cup apple cider vinegar

2 cups cream or light
sour cream or low-fat
natural yoghurt

2 cloves garlic, crushed

2 tablespoons chopped fresh
parsley

1 tablespoon snipped fresh
chives

½ teaspoon freshly ground
black pepper, or to taste

½ teaspoon salt, or to taste

grated rind and juice of
½ lemon

Mix all ingredients gently together in a mixing bowl until evenly combined. Pour into a covered container and refrigerate for at least 3 hours or overnight, to allow the flavours to blend.

Store extra dressing in the refrigerator for up to 3 days.

Typing this recipe brings back memories of my Mum's favourite salad dressing. Or, should I say, my favourite dressing that Mum used to make. It was very simple: a cup of whipped cream, a few tablespoons of French mustard folded in, cracked black pepper and very little salt. Just before she served it she would add about two or three tablespoons of wine vinegar. Things don't change much, do they?

In our endless quest of finding another housekeeper like our Jackie we tried one girl who was willing, but couldn't cook. We had such a bad run of cooks that season, who all said they could cook but couldn't, so we thought, what the hell, take one who says she can't cook – we might be pleasantly surprised!

Well, she couldn't cook, but she was willing to learn and was a fast learner. Marlee taught her how to make our summer salad. After two or three attempts under supervision she was confident enough to make it alone. One day Franz came into the kitchen and he noticed she was adding the oil too fast, not whisking enough and, of course, the mixture separated.

Franz, being Franz, decided to have a bit of fun, and maintaining a serious expression said, 'Did Marlee tell you the salad dressing can only be made on the day of a full moon? Also, if you don't stir the mixture in an anticlockwise direction the oil and vinegar will always separate?'

'Oooooh, no, Marlee didn't tell me that,' she replied in a very concerned manner. 'What am I going to do?'

'Well, you will just have to wait for the next full moon.'

'Will this come right if I stir it correctly then?'

With a serious expression, Franz replied 'No, I would say this is ruined. We will just have to use it the way it is.'

She immediately rushed to the calendar to see the date of the next full moon and made a note, 'make salad dressing'.

'Oh, by the way, in the northern hemisphere you have to stir clockwise.' Franz walked out of the kitchen with a smile.

The next week when we were out of salad and Marlee told the cook to make some more, she got the reply, 'I can't, I have to wait for the full moon.'

Marlee was told the story of the full moon, the cook didn't speak to Franz for a while and she certainly didn't believe anything else he ever said. She would rush to someone else and check on every statement he made if it was something she needed an answer about.

So much for salad dressings.

As I mentioned earlier, we need to drink a lot in January. Sometimes we replace meals with a health drink. I've listed some of our favourites below.

Health Drinks

Start the day with a zing!

1 mango, peeled and stoned
2 oranges, peeled and sliced
1 cup milk
¼ cup natural yoghurt
1 banana, peeled and thickly sliced
2 tablespoons lemon juice
¼ cup wheatgerm
2 tablespoons honey
8 ice cubes

Combine all the ingredients in a blender or food processor and mix until smooth. Feed the ice cubes in 2 at a time, for a better blend. Serve immediately in chilled glasses.

Serves 3 – 4

A health drink to take regularly.

1 cup pearl barley
2 litres boiling water
6 oranges
3 lemons

Add barley to boiling water in a large pan and simmer, covered, for 1 hour.

Strain and reserve barley water; keep the barley. Add the grated rind of 2 oranges and 2 lemons to the barley water. Stand until cool.

Peel oranges and lemons and put the fruit into a blender or food processor with the reserved barley. Process until smooth. Add to the barley water. Mix well. Cover and chill in the refrigerator.

Serve cold in tall glasses. Store remaining 'health drink' in refrigerator.

Serves 10 – 12

I love this one taken from an old recipe book, dated 1829, in the American South.

'To Be Taken By Anyone Suspected of Going Into a Decline.'
'½ pint warm milk, warm from the cow, made lusciously sweet
with old conserve of roses and a shot of the very best rum.
Take it first thing in the morning.'
(NB. ½ pint in American = a scant Australian 250 ml metric cup)

I suspect that most of the population was suspecting to go into a decline!

We live on fruit smoothies in January! These delicious, icy concoctions are often consumed during the daytime in the hot months. Made with fresh bananas, these smoothies are very creamy tasting but are low in kilojoules and have zero fat! A combination of any seasonal fruit is good.

Fruit Smoothies

1 banana, peeled

2 peaches, peeled and stoned

1 nectarine, stones

10 strawberries, hulled

2 mangoes, peeled and stoned

1 apple, peeled, cored and sliced

1 orange, peeled and sliced

1 pear, peeled, cored and sliced

or whatever is in season and plentiful

Combine a mixture of prepared seasonal fruits in a blender until smooth.

After blending the fruits together until smooth, pour mixture into ice cube trays and freeze until firm.

To make a smoothie, take 6 to 8 frozen cubes (depending on size); put into a blender. Add 1 fresh peeled banana and mix together until smooth and creamy. This method makes a very creamy fruit smoothie. You would think the mixture had cream in it! Serve in a tall chilled glass.

SERVES UP TO 6 PEOPLE

I thought I'd finish the chapter with the delicious slice that finished our New Year's Eve feast. It is very naughty, but sometimes in life you have to be naughty for no rhyme or reason and I thought New Year's Eve was the time!

Lemon and Raisin Slice

Pastry:

1 cup plain flour

1 cup self-raising flour

½ cup cornflour

¼ cup custard powder

¼ cup icing sugar

185 g butter

⅓ cup water, approximately

3 teaspoons lemon juice

Filling:

½ cup apricot jam

90 g unsalted butter

¼ cup caster sugar

2 eggs, separated

½ cup chopped seedless raisins

2 teaspoons grated lemon rind

250 g cottage cheese, sieved

¼ cup light sour cream

egg yolk for glazing

To make pastry: Sift together all the dry ingredients into a mixing bowl. Add butter and rub in until the mixture resembles fine breadcrumbs.

Mix to a firm dough, not mushy, by adding sufficient water and lemon juice (lean towards the lemon juice, for flavour) and mix with a round-bladed knife. Tip the dough onto a lightly floured surface and knead lightly.

To make filling: Cream butter and sugar until light and fluffy. Add egg yolks, raisins, lemon rind, cottage cheese and sour cream. Mix well. Whisk egg whites in a clean, polished bowl until stiff; fold into lemon and raisin mixture.

To finish slice: Divide the dough in half; roll out one half to a rectangle and line a lightly greased lamington tin. Spread the dough with apricot jam then the filling.

Roll out the remaining dough and place on top of the filling. Trim edges of dough and brush the top with beaten egg yolk.

Bake in a moderate oven/185°C, for 35 to 40 minutes, until golden brown. Stand tin on a wire cooling rack; cool. When cool, cut into slices and sift icing sugar over the top.

MAKES 18 – 24 SLICES

February

Speck

~

Mushroom and Olive Salad

~

Barra in Beer Sauce with Crunchy Topping

~

Raw Barra in Marinade

~

Chicken and Corn Soup

~

Beef Jerky

~

Boiled Tongue

~

Spaghetti Bolognaise, Bullo-Style

~

oliday time!

Under the 'Charlie regime' holidays were only considered necessary if you were on the verge of collapse and there was some money to spare.

Everyone, except for Charlie, was always on the verge of collapse from just putting up with him and there was never any money, let alone 'spare' money.

So you had to be a stretcher case before you could get away from Bullo.

The children and I did manage to go on a few holidays over the years. But five years without a break was not out of the ordinary at Bullo. At one stage I didn't leave the station to go shopping, to see the doctor, to go to town or visit a neighbour for eighteen months!

But, I am happy to say, I have changed that situation for the better. A few years ago we began to take a holiday every year in February! The crops are planted, the rains have really settled in for the season, the grass is green and the cattle are getting fat. Little baby everythings are running and romping and flying everywhere in and out of the rain. It's time for R & R!

Our first holiday in years was to Austria and now it has become our favourite destination. Franz sees his family and friends while Marlee and I learn all about Austria and meet everyone. We see all we can, weather permitting.

We do different, exciting things like skiing (or try to), enjoy the cool change (15°C below zero!), and travel to so many interesting places and countries.

A trip to Darwin from Bullo is 1200 kilometres and in all that distance we pass one major town (well, major for the Territory) and half a dozen rather small stops.

In a 1200 kilometre trip from Franz's village in Austria, you can visit Germany, Italy, France, Belgium, Poland, Switzerland and Hungary and it would take a book to list the towns you could visit. You see some of the best art galleries, museums and historic sites in the world, not to mention the amazing evidence of past history.

To get to Franz's village, the highway passes through a valley in the Alps. Running alongside this modern highway is a road built by the Romans, on their journey through the Alps. Coming from a country like Australia with only two hundred years of white settlement, I found it fascinating. The locals grow up surrounded by and steeped in this history, so they treat a road built by the Romans as a normal part of the landscape. I suppose when your local village church is nine hundred years old, you tend to be complacent!

At Bullo we have to keep reminding ourselves that most people don't have a quarter of a million hectares as their backyards. So I suppose it is all relative.

The other major excitement when visiting Austria is sampling all the wonderful food. You are surrounded by delicious food on all sides, both inside and outside the country. So many of the wonderful foods are now readily available in Australia, due to Europeans coming to live here, and the famous recipes of nearly every country of the world are now available in print.

But there are some traditional foods that are very hard to get outside a small village in any country. One of these foods that I have become addicted to is Speck (a wonderful Austrian smoked meat that is a cross between ham and bacon). The Speck is usually homemade and Franz's family, like most of the people in the village, make their own Speck.

Food is a very social thing, no more obvious anywhere than it is the small villages of Europe. There is great competition each year to see who makes the best Speck. There is much visitation, sampling, discussion and comment before coming to the final decision. But it is never really a final verdict; the discussions just continue until the village's next batch is made and the judging starts all over again.

I would say without a doubt, no discussion needed, that the best Speck in Obermillstat has to be made by the Ranacher family. I couldn't stop eating it, Marlee was the same, and Franz, having been away for a few years, was right up there with us. The village can appoint me 'Speck judge' anytime!

I am putting the recipe in here, just to show you why it can't be bought at the corner store. It can only be made in a very few cold, dry parts of Australia, so you will probably have to visit Austria if you want to sample Speck.

I asked Franz how old the recipe was. He had no idea, but said it was in the book of records in the village church. This means it has to be at least nine hundred years old!

Speck

You need 1 whole medium pig, about 120 kg – the idea is to have young, lean, tender meat

Leave the skin on and completely bone the pig.

Lay the deboned pig meat flat on a large tray and dry-cure with salt, lots of crushed garlic, ground black peppercorns and a mixture of spices such as caraway seeds and grated nutmeg.

Leave for 2 weeks in a refrigerator or an icy-cold cellar (in Austria), before smoking.

Smoke for 2 weeks, all day and most of the night. The wood you use for smoking is important. Use oak, maple or any other hard wood. It must be cold smoked, below 40°C.

Dry out for 3 or 4 months, or longer if you wish, in the cold cellar. Make sure the place is cool and dry or the outside of the speck goes mouldy.

Speck is served sliced paper thin, with homemade rye bread, mild chillies, sweet-and-sour gherkins or pickled cucumbers and a good cheese. Franz says Emmental is the one he likes best.

It is just as well we only visit Austria for four weeks because Speck is just one of many foods that send my fat intake to new highs.

Austria must have the most amazing array of delicious, very fattening cakes and desserts that I have ever seen. The displays in the coffee houses are mouth-watering, full of amazing desserts or cakes, such as the world-famous Sacher Torte. Austria also is home to many more dishes such as Wiener Schnitzel, equally delicious and high in fat, and the bread could be a meal on its own.

You would need to walk ten kilometres a day, uphill on skis, just to work off your daily fat consumption. We would love to stay much longer than the four short weeks but we would need to control our eating habits!

February often finds me writing in many different places around the world; in fact every other year seems to find me on a working holiday. Some years I write from 5.00 am to midday, then I have the afternoons to enjoy the scenery and the food.

Food becomes a main focus on holiday because I have the time to sit over meals and enjoy what I am eating. I am drawn to foods that the weather on Bullo prevents us from eating. Butter, chocolates and cream melt at room temperature for most of the year on Bullo. So it is a treat to be able to sit at a table with butter and cake and not see them both melt into two greasy puddles within minutes.

I remember a non-holiday February when Marlee and I didn't leave the station and we were craving something sweet so Marlee decided to make a delicious creamy concoction. She had to assemble the cake in the chiller, because the day was so hot, then semi freeze it just to keep it together. The weather didn't improve — it was still blistering hot after sunset — and we were inundated with thousands of bugs in the build-up to a horrendous storm that finally arrived at two in the morning. So we sat in the chiller, in the dark, with a cold beer each and ate our cake!

As well as eating food that is as cold as possible, we also try to work in our favourite recipes, because the pace of life allows time to talk and enjoy the food and company. We love our favourite green salad (see recipe on page 24), but because we eat salad every day during the hot months, we sometimes like a change. The following salad is another favourite.

Mushroom and Olive Salad

250 g fresh button or small cup mushrooms

150 g mixed black and green olives, pitted

1 red capsicum, seeded and chopped

6 spring onions/shallots, thinly sliced

½ cup chopped fresh parsley

1 cup Summer Anchovy Dressing (recipe page 26)

Clean mushrooms by brushing with a soft brush – a clean pastry brush is ideal – and trim stalks. Leave mushrooms whole.

Combine mushrooms, olives, capsicum, spring onions and parsley in an attractive serving bowl. Add dressing; toss gently. Cover and refrigerate for at least 1 hour, then serve.

SERVES 6 – 8

Seafood also ranks high on the list of favourites, on or off the station. On the station we have an endless supply of fresh barramundi and Franz and Marlee are tops at fishing. So we never eat barra off the property. No-one could serve barra as fresh as we get on Bullo: fresh out of the river, a kilometre down the airstrip from the homestead, delivered by motorbike straight into the frying pan.

Many, many years ago, my wonderful Mary taught me to cook fish on the river bank, particularly with the hook still in its mouth. She'd haul the barra onto the mud banks using a bent nail tied to a piece of string. Then, without gutting or scaling the fish, she'd cover it in mud or leaves (depending on what was available) and chuck the whole thing into the fire, poking continually at the coals and fish with a stick. When it was ready she would dig around in the coals and peel back a charred mess to reveal the whitest of fish flesh, minus skin and scales. My first taste of barra cooked the Aboriginal way was out of this world. However, its preparation certainly left a lot to be desired!

I started taking along a few items from the kitchen on our fishing afternoons and the rest of the group would watch as the invisible struggle of wills between Mary and me continued. It took a long time to get her to even gut the fish and then I had to move very slowly into the adding of a few herbs and flavourings. But I finally had a fish tasting out of this world, gutted and flavoured with lemon juice, ginger and some parsley. No matter how hard I tried, I could never get soy sauce anywhere near the fish. I don't know what Mary had against soy sauce, but whatever it was it was significant, so the soy sauce stayed back in the kitchen. I managed to get in some garlic when she wasn't looking and then Mary took over, covered everything in mud, went through the poking routine and 'hey presto', a cooked barra appeared.

The girls and I waited as Mary ceremoniously tested my variation on her fish. Mary's remark about our joint cooking effort was, 'good tucker, Missus!' I officially became a registered member of the fishing club and was invited on the afternoon fishing excursions with all the women, on a regular basis.

On Bullo we usually cook barra in a plain and simple fashion. There are some recipes in other months for barra, but the following is a fancy way to prepare it.

Barra in Beer Sauce with Crunchy Topping

1 kg barramundi fillets
or similar

½ teaspoon rock salt

2 cups beer

6 spring onions/shallots,
thinly sliced

½ lemon, thinly sliced

1 bay leaf

12 grinds freshly ground
black pepper

2 tablespoons butter

3 teaspoons cornflour

2 teaspoons sugar

Crunchy Topping:

2 tablespoons olive oil

1 cup fresh breadcrumbs

½ cup chopped fresh parsley

2 cloves garlic, crushed

Sprinkle barramundi fillets with rock salt and let stand for 20 minutes.

Cut fillets into serving sizes; place in a heavy-based frying pan with the beer, spring onions, lemon and bay leaf. Sprinkle with freshly ground black pepper.

Place pan over a medium heat and bring to the boil; reduce to low and simmer for around 15 minutes. Remove the fish from the pan and place on a warm serving plate. Keep warm.

Mix the butter and cornflour together to make a paste. Add gradually to the pan, stirring constantly. Add sugar and stir for 3 minutes, or until smooth. Pour sauce over the fish.

To make Crunchy Topping: Heat olive oil in a small pan over a medium heat; add breadcrumbs, parsley and garlic and stir until crunchy.

Sprinkle the topping over the fish just before serving.

SERVES 4

Opposite: Speck (recipe page 36) with Emmental cheese and beer. Following pages: Barra in Beer Sauce with Crunchy Topping (recipe this page).

If I get off the station in February, I tend to eat lots of seafood (other than barra of course): crabs, oysters, clams, scallops and octopus. They all must be as fresh and as simply cooked as possible. I also eat as much sashimi as I can, whenever I am near a good Japanese restaurant.

It is not a short or easy journey to get to a good Japanese restaurant from Bullo, in fact it is a 1200 kilometre journey. And it is even harder to get the right fish for sashimi into Bullo. So, until we hit the 'big smoke' we use the following recipe as a substitute.

Raw Barra in Marinade

Great for summer meals with salads.

1 kg barramundi fillets or similar white fish fillets with no bones and firm flesh

grated rind and juice of 4 lemons

grated rind and juice of 1 orange

grated rind and juice of 2 limes

2 lemons, thinly sliced, with all seeds removed

8 grinds freshly ground black pepper

¼ teaspoon salt

3 Spanish red or white onions, very thinly sliced

chopped fresh herbs for garnish

Slice the barramundi fillets into thin slices, about 0.5 cm thick and 5 cm in length.

In a small bowl, combine the lemon rind, orange rind and lime rind. Mix gently. Combine the lemon juice, orange juice and lime juice in a jug.

Line a large glass dish with half of the fish slices. Pour in half of the mixed juice; sprinkle with half the mixed rind, half the freshly ground black pepper and salt. Put a layer of sliced lemon and a layer of sliced onion on top of the fish. Repeat this process with the remaining fish. Make sure the liquid covers the top layer of the fish. Add more juice if necessary.

Cover the dish and place in the coldest part of the refrigerator for 24 hours.

Serve barra in marinade sprinkled with chopped fresh herbs; accompany with a mixed green salad.

SERVES 4 – 6

Opposite: Pumpkin Chiffon Pie (recipe page 64) with Maple-Glazed Pecans (recipe page 65).

Storms keep rolling in, rain comes in torrential waves of water, the heavens rumble and vibrate and thunder explodes in deafening cracks. The storms settle in the valley, nestling in between the mountain ranges. This frightening display of awesome power usually happens right over the top of the homestead!

The poor old lightning conductor works overtime and on more than one occasion during the rainy season, it has given up the ghost completely and just exploded.

The torrential rain settles in, causing a complete 'white-out' of the entire valley. Electrical discharges rapidly jump from cloud to cloud in harmony with the thunderclaps. Chain lightning runs for kilometres through clouds, eventually colliding with more lightning, igniting and sending an amazing display of chain lightning hurtling toward earth. The combined energy is so powerful it incinerates anything in its path. Trees just vanish in massive explosions, leaving nothing but a smouldering charred heap. These horrific storms cause lots of damage, as well as lots of extra, dangerous work.

The only way to travel around the station during the wet is by horse, so after one of these violent storms moves on, you need to go out to check everything. If the storm has caused flooding cattle need to be moved from the lower paddocks.

These storms move at amazing speeds. Many times we have been out moving cattle, before the storm is due to hit, only to get caught right in the middle of it. Before the storm arrives you are sweltering in temperatures of 40°C plus and your clothes stuck to you with sweat. Sweat drops off the ends of your hair and runs down your back – you think it can't possibly get any hotter. Fortunately, the cattle you are moving feel exactly the same – this is the one time of the year that you seem to have direct communication. The rest of the year you chase them up hills, over rocks and through creeks. The last thing they will do is what you want. But in February they are very obliging. You open a gate and ask them to go through and they do. Everyone and every animal is intent on just finishing what has to be done so they can get out of the sun to somewhere cool.

Then the storm arrives, ahead of schedule. The temperature plummets from the mid-forties to the low twenties as a dense black cloud rolls into the valley and you brace yourself for the turmoil of dust, wind and debris that precedes the rain. One minute you are choking and sneezing, gasping for breath in the dust, then suddenly you are plunged from sweating, seething heat into teeth-chattering, needle-sharp, freezing rain. When your body is plunged from 40° plus to around 20° in seconds the reaction is quite violent. It takes quite a while for the teeth to stop chattering and for the body to stop shaking.

Many years ago, one such storm caught Charlie and the girls out in the lower paddocks moving cattle to higher ground. I waited back at the homestead, unable to do anything, watching down the road in the direction of the paddocks, praying that the silhouettes of horses and riders would come over the ridge. Finally, three very cold and wet riders eased themselves out of their saddles at the back gate.

This day the storm had come out of nowhere, so they hadn't taken a coat, thinking they would be back in the homestead long before the storm even arrived.

When I say they were freezing cold – they were freezing cold! Their skin was as cold as ice. I grabbed the two little girls and said, 'Quickly, out of the wet clothes and into a hot shower, now. Mummy will make you some lovely hot chicken soup.'

Two little faces looked up at me – lips blue, teeth uncontrollably chattering, bodies shaking.

I went into the kitchen to heat up the frozen chicken soup. We had no such thing as a microwave – the most modern appliance was an electric fridge with a freezer. I had to be selective about what I could freeze because of the limited space (half the freezer was taken up with ice cubes), but there was always a container of chicken soup.

I thawed the block slowly over low heat and hurried into the living room with the steaming hot soup.

The girls were sitting with Charlie. They were in dry clothes and had stopped shaking. They smiled up at me, incapable of any movement and unable to take the soup bowls I offered.

'What have you done to them!' I screamed at Charlie.

'Nothing. I just gave them a Hot Toddy, to warm them up,' said Charlie, with a hurt tone to his voice. Then, when he realised he'd done the wrong thing, he feebly added 'Look, they're not shaking.'

'They're drunk!' I fumed. 'How much rum did you give them?'

I won't go into what else I said, but believe me, Charlie didn't get a chance to say one word. I doubt if he was capable of conversation. The three faces just smiled up at me, frantically trying to keep their eyes in focus.

The girls were very sick. Eventually, after their stomachs heaved up the terrible concoction that Charlie had fed them, I was able to get some hot chicken soup into them. School was out and they suffered terrible hangovers the next day.

Whenever I cook chicken soup I think of Charlie and his 'Hot Toddy'. It also reminds me of Mum – when I was growing up it was one of her cures (as well as Bex powders). The chicken soup memories will never fade.

The following recipe is a combination of both my Bullo recipe and Auntie Sue's recipe. It's my very favourite soup.

Chicken and Corn Soup

2 large, single, skinless chicken breast fillets

2 egg whites

1 litre chicken stock, preferably homemade

1 tablespoon cornflour

3 tablespoons water

1 x 200 g can sweetcorn kernels, drained and rinsed or 1 cup fresh corn kernels

4 tablespoons fresh green peas

salt

3 tablespoons dry sherry

1 teaspoon sesame oil

25 g cooked ham, (optional)

lots of chopped fresh parsley

Finely chop the chicken flesh until it is almost a mush. The food processor does this well. Place in a bowl; add egg whites and mix thoroughly.

Bring the chicken stock to the boil in a large pan. Meanwhile, blend cornflour smoothly with water, in a small bowl.

Add the corn and cornflour mixture to the pan; bring back to the boil, stirring constantly.

When the mixture reboils, gradually stir in the chicken mixture. Stirring gently, add the peas, salt to taste, sherry and sesame oil. Simmer for 15 minutes over a medium–low heat.

Chop the ham finely. Pour the soup into a soup tureen or individual soup bowls and garnish with chopped ham and lots and lots of chopped parsley.

SERVES 4 – 6

February gives us the time we need to cook the time-consuming recipes. During February our bodies still need more salt and the best way to get the salt intake into your body (salt tablets are a 'no-no') is to eat 'salt meat'.

Salt meat – what memories these two words conjure up! Until I went to Bullo I had never set eyes on a piece of 'salt meat' – I didn't even know such a thing existed. So when I was asked to cook it I was at a loss. I asked the manager what to do and the reply was along these lines, 'Chuck it in the pot with some water and whatever else you can find.' Remember, this was way back in 1962 when I didn't even know how to light a wood stove!

I approached the vile-looking, dried-up lump on the table and pondered the instructions. I found a large saucepan without any holes (a major feat in those days) and filled it with water, dropped the horrible lump in and proceeded to look for the 'anything else you can find' part of the recipe. I put in some potatoes, a variety of dried vegetables, seasoned it with salt, and let it cook away merrily for many hours.

To say it tasted vile was the understatement of the century. We got our week's supply of salt in the first mouthful! I then learned, or should I say was told, that you must wash the salt meat, many times, and change the cooking water as many times in the first hour of cooking, before you settle down and add the vegetables, etc. And you don't season with salt.

It was then I decided I had to conquer this cooking jazz. Instead of dry salt beef we now corn our beef, make a delicious boiled tongue and our own beef jerky. They are all far tastier methods of preserving beef than the first lump of salt meat I encountered thirty-five years ago.

When the girls were away at boarding school I received letter after letter from them saying how terrible the food was. I took pity on them and started sending relief packages. In one of them I put some beef jerky. The requests for more came at an alarming pace; I even received phone calls asking for increased shipments!

The truth was soon revealed: they had a thriving business selling the jerky to all the 'city slickers' who had never seen or tasted it before. The headmistress was horrified, but I thought it showed good business sense. However, they were not allowed to receive any more large shipments of jerky. Here is the recipe if you would like to try making it yourself.

Beef Jerky

Use beef with no fat.
One of the best cuts is a
round of beef.

Slice beef to the thickness of 2 rashers of sliced bacon. (It is easier to slice thinly if beef is semi-frozen.) Arrange the sliced beef in the bottom of a shallow glass or porcelain dish. Sprinkle with a coating of cooking salt to cover completely then grind black peppercorns over all of the beef to make a generous coating. Turn all the beef slices over and repeat the process with more salt and freshly ground black pepper. Cover and leave in the refrigerator for 24 hours.

Thread the beef slices onto a length of butcher's twine; hang in a cool place such as a coolroom or an icy cold cellar in the draught of a fan, and dry for 2 days, or until meat is dried right through. There must be no evidence of fat or lumps of moist meat.

This is a very simple, but tasty beef jerky. It is best made in the cold months of the year. If made in warmer months, it can be dried in a cold air-conditioned room in a current of cold air created by the fan. If the beef gets sweaty it is no good! It is very handy to take on a muster for a sustaining, nourishing snack. It is also great for bushwalking and camping.

EDITOR'S NOTE: If access to a coolroom, an icy cold cellar or an air-conditioned room is not available, the following alternative method is suggested for small quantities of beef to give a safe result.

After salting and refrigerating the beef slices for 24 hours, according to the above method, arrange them on wire cooling racks, in a single layer, and place in a very low oven/80°C for 2 hours, to dry out. Remove the beef slices from the oven (they will be semi-dry) and place, uncovered, in the refrigerator, so that the cold dry air can complete the drying process.

I am surprised how many people don't realise that the colouring used in corned beef is produced by poison. And it is not just the city people that are not aware. Most people on the land know about salt and corned meat, but not all as I found out.

Way back when the girls were too young to build fences, Charlie hired contractors to do the job. One season a team of three arrived to work on building new paddocks. They were working about twenty miles from the homestead so were camping out and we didn't expect to see them until the job was done. Their boss settled them in and then he went off to another job on a nearby station.

The contractors arrived back at the homestead after two days, complaining that they were dying – they did look very sick. I called the medical service on the radio and the doctor went through a field of questions. He said to keep them resting, to watch for any change and to call back daily.

I put them all to bed in the temporary Bullo hospital ward and tended my patients. By the next morning they were much improved but the doctor said to wait another day before they went bush again. When the boss arrived the following day he wouldn't believe they had been sick and he sent them all back to the bush. The boss watched them for a day and then off he went again. Three days later they were back again, crawling into my kitchen in a near state of collapse.

The doctor was mystified; he asked question after question. He thought it might be the water they were drinking causing the sickness, so it was decided they would take water from the house when they went again. After three days or so their health improved. Off they went with their water, but in three days were back again and this time they were really sick. The boss arrived at the same time as his team at the back gate and he saw that indeed, they looked 'a mite seedy'.

I sat them down and went through everything they had done from the moment they had left the homestead. They were sick out in the bush, but they got better the moment they came back to the homestead.

The solution, like with most things, was discovered by accident. One of the men came out of the bathroom after a shower and remarked, 'Well, at least my hair is not falling out by the handful now.'

My ears pricked up and I got straight on the radio to the doctor, 'Yes,' he replied, 'your suspicions are correct. If their hair is falling out then they definitely sound as if they are being poisoned.'

We sat down and went through what they were eating. It turned out they were boiling most of their meat and to make it a pretty colour the one cooking was putting a fistful of saltpetre in the water, each time.

It had been a long time since I had used saltpetre – about twenty years – but I vaguely remembered the measurement was something like one tablespoon to five kilograms of salt for curing meat. You never cook with it. The men were adding about fifty times the correct amount and were poisoning themselves at a very fast rate!

Here is our recipe for Boiled Tongue. Not requiring saltpetre it is a much safer alternative to corned beef!

Boiled Tongue

1 beef tongue, fresh
not salted

2 cups red wine or
dry sherry

1 tablespoon cracked black
pepper

1 tablespoon salt

1 tablespoon brown sugar
or honey

1 onion, cut in wedges

2 cloves garlic, crushed

Scrub the tongue under running cold water. Place tongue in a large pan or boiler. Add wine, pepper, salt, sugar, onion and garlic. Add enough cold water to this mixture to cover the tongue.

Cover pan and bring slowly to the boil over a medium heat. Reduce to medium-low and simmer tongue for approximately 2 hours or until tender. Test with a fine metal skewer.

Remove the pan from the heat and let the tongue cool in the liquid. When cool, remove tongue from pan and peel off the outer skin. Remove any bones and gristle.

Slice the tongue very thinly and serve cold with cranberry sauce or fruit chutney and salads, or use it in sandwiches.

SERVES 6 – 8

Many of the recipes in this book bring back memories and as soon as I looked at Bullo's spaghetti bolognaise the memories certainly came flooding back.

I was taught to make this dish in the Philippines. When I arrived in Manila in 1960 I was sick, pregnant and we were living on the sailing boat. A friend of Charlie's visited us on board, saw I wasn't faring too well and offered us an apartment. We moved into air-conditioned bliss.

I later found out Charlie's friend was, I suppose you would say, a modern-day gangster who ran illegal gambling casinos. The apartment he let us use was his girlfriend's place, so you could say were 'holed-up in a gangster's moll's joint!'

After spending three blissful months there, Charlie managed to find us an apartment of our own and I didn't have to return to life on the rolling waves.

I met the owner of the apartment and she was a delightful person. You would never guess her lifestyle just by looking at her. We had lunch together in her apartment and she served me spaghetti bolognaise. I said how delicious it was and then I got the story of why she was so good at making bolognaise.

Before her career in Manila, she lived in the Bronx in New York, where she was married to an Italian with a great love of food and an extremely violent temper. He taught her to make bolognaise, but she was not a good cook and apparently was a slow learner.

If she didn't make the dish to his standard, he would 'Beat the s - - - out of me!' (to put it in her words). So she quickly learned to make bolognaise to his liking and then she left him. A few months of this kind of tucker and she could have put her Italian husband in his place!

Here is her spaghetti bolognaise recipe, via Manila, via New York! We now claim it as our very own Spaghetti Bolognaise, Bullo-Style.

Spaghetti Bolognaise, Bullo-Style

100 g bacon, finely chopped

3 tablespoons olive oil

3 large onions, finely chopped

1 carrot, finely chopped

1 stalk celery, finely chopped

6 large cloves garlic, crushed

1 kg finely minced lean beef

1 tablespoon soy sauce

3 x 425 g cans tomatoes
or 1.5 kg fresh tomatoes,
chopped

½ cup tomato paste

500 g mushrooms, sliced

10 g dried mushrooms,
soaked in boiling water for
10 minutes, drained and
sliced

1 teaspoon dried basil or
1 tablespoon chopped
fresh basil

1 teaspoon dried oregano or
1 tablespoon chopped
fresh oregano

1 teaspoon grated or ground
nutmeg

5 cups red wine

1 beef stock cube

1 chicken stock cube

1 tablespoon butter (optional)

800 g – 1 kg spaghetti

½ cup cream

salt and freshly ground black
pepper to taste

chopped fresh parsley for
garnish

125 g parmesan cheese,
freshly grated

Heat a large heavy-based pan over a medium–high heat, add bacon and cook, stirring occasionally, until crunchy. Place bacon on a plate.

Add 1 tablespoon oil to pan and gently fry onions, carrot, celery and garlic over a medium heat, stirring occasionally, until vegetables start to brown, about 5 to 7 minutes. Add vegetables to bacon.

Brown minced beef in pan in 3 batches, adding remaining oil gradually with each batch. Return all beef to pan; sprinkle with soy sauce.

Return bacon and vegetables to pan. Add tomatoes, tomato paste, mushrooms, basil, oregano, nutmeg, wine and stock cubes to pan. Bring to the boil, stirring frequently. Reduce to medium-low; cover and simmer for at least 1 hour, or more because the longer you simmer it, the better the flavour.

Fifteen minutes before serving, add butter (if liked). Simmer without lid for the last 15 minutes, to reduce and thicken the sauce.

Meanwhile, cook spaghetti in lots of boiling salted water in a large pan or boiler, until tender but still firm, about 10 minutes. Drain well. Place in a large warm serving bowl; sprinkle with parsley. Stir cream into sauce; season to taste with salt and pepper. Serve in a warm serving bowl; sprinkle with some parmesan cheese. Serve remaining cheese in a small bowl. Serve immediately, with garlic or herb bread and green salad.

SERVES 8 – 10

March

Marlee's Beef Stroganoff

≈

Marlee's Orange Chocolate Mousse

≈

Bullo River Beef Stew

≈

Bullo-Style Cabbage

≈

Bullo River Pot Roast

≈

Apple Cream Cinnamon Cake

≈

Pumpkin Chiffon Pie

≈

Maple-Glazed Pecans

≈

Mango Chicken, Bullo-Style

≈

By March you feel a change in temperature (be it ever so slight) from the previous months. In the heat of the north even a few degrees is a welcome change. Bullo welcomes us home from our holidays with rolling green pastures as far as the eye can see.

Of course for the first few days back from Austria it is like walking into a blast furnace, until our bodies readjust to the temperatures of the north. The few degrees make such a difference. The dogs are no longer collapsed against the door of the air-conditioned office, begging to get in, or pressing their noses against the crack between the door and floor, sucking in every drop of the escaping cold air. They are out exploring.

Having been convinced we had deserted them forever, their joy at our return is evident. Sumie, having only five centimetres of tail, tries to wag it so hard that she falls over. Mr Mustang keeps up a strange whine yelp howl type of noise. He runs around in circles chasing his tail until either Franz shouts at him or he falls over. It takes days for them to calm down and the greeting is repeated hourly. Mr Mustang will suddenly launch himself into Franz's arms and start up the long torturous howl, while looking lovingly into his eyes.

Sumie is much more refined and just never lets me out of her sight. She does lapse, every now and then, by trying to sit in my lap. Munro pokes and nudges me regularly just to see if I'm real and seems compelled to lick me all over.

After a few days they realise we are there to stay, so they settle back to their normal, over-affectionate selves. The dogs can sense the excitement in the air. The new season is about to begin and they join in the preparations with gusto.

We are still looking for cooling foods during the day, but as the night approaches and the temperature starts to creep slowly down, more substantial foods come to mind.

The following is one of Marlee's specialities.

Marlee's Beef Stroganoff

If you use a good quality non-stick frying pan for this dish, you can reduce the butter to 60 g.

2 kg fillet or rump beef steak,
cut into strips

125 g butter

2 onions, thinly sliced

2 large cloves garlic, crushed

20 large mushrooms, sliced

⅓ cup tomato paste

2 cups red wine

1 cup white wine vinegar

4 tablespoons French or
wholegrain mustard

2 beef stock cubes, crumbled

freshly ground black pepper
to taste

1 cup sour cream or low-fat
yoghurt

In a large, heavy-based, hot frying pan, cook the beef strips in small amounts, over a medium-high heat, using some of the butter with each lot, until well browned. Set beef aside and keep warm.

Then add the onions and garlic to the pan and cook over a medium heat until golden brown. Add the mushrooms; cook gently for a few minutes, stirring occasionally.

Add tomato paste, wine, vinegar, mustard, stock cubes and pepper to taste. Stir until boiling. Reduce heat to medium-low and simmer for 2 minutes. If sauce reduces too much, add some water or chicken stock. If sauce is not thick enough, add a mixture of cornflour blended with water to a smooth paste, and return to the boil, stirring constantly.

Add the beef to the sauce and stir until heated through. When ready to serve, fold in the sour cream; stir a few times to heat through but do not boil. Serve immediately. Delicious with rice, buttered noodles or boiled potatoes tossed in parsley, minted fresh peas or other green vegetables and a green salad.

SERVES 8

In March we often miss the sweet foods that we ate in Austria Below is a favourite dessert that satisfies these cravings. Try it when you feel like something sweet – you don't need a special occasion as a reason to indulge.

Marlee's Orange Chocolate Mousse

500 g dark chocolate

175 g unsalted butter

9 large eggs, separated

¾ cup caster sugar

grated rind of 2 oranges

3 tablespoons strained fresh orange juice

3 tablespoons orange-flavoured liqueur, such as Grand Marnier

600 ml thickened cream, whipped

extra chocolate, cream and strawberries for decoration

Melt chocolate in the top of a double-boiler over gently bubbling water. Stir in butter until melted and smooth; remove from heat and leave to cool.

In a large bowl, beat egg yolks with ¼ cup sugar until fluffy. Add orange rind, orange juice, liqueur and chocolate mixture. Mix gently to combine.

Whisk egg whites in a large, clean polished bowl, with an electric mixer on high speed, until stiff. Add remaining sugar gradually, whisking constantly.

Fold egg whites and whipped cream into chocolate mixture, cutting and folding gently, until mixture is smooth.

Pour mixture into attractive individual serving dishes and chill.

When ready to serve, decorate each with chocolate curls, a dollop of whipped cream and a sliced strawberry.

Serves 12

Opposite: A typical muster lunch. Packed sandwiches and Mum's Spicy Gingercake (recipe page 209) topped with Lemon-Lime Butter Icing (recipe page 78). Following page: Bullo River Beef Stew (recipe page 58) with Bullo-Style Cabbage (recipe page 60).

The memories of stew are some of my earlier ones. Stew is the backbone of the 'station' cook's menu – if fact, for some of them it is their entire menu!

The first so-called 'cook' I met at Bullo was actually a saddler/horse tailer (a person who took care of the horses when out on muster, back in the old days) who cooked in his spare time. Stew was his only meal, apart from when he excelled himself and served me boiled, stuffed ox heart for Christmas lunch!

I grew up eating Mum's cooking and everything she cooked was delicious, especially her stews. So when I first set eyes on the mess the saddler served as stew, I was horrified: boiled salt meat; grey, dirty water bubbling away, with grease floating on top; and potatoes, not peeled or washed, so all the dirt was gaily bubbling around with the rest of the mess.

His stews were served with a soup ladle – this man knew nothing about thickening. His idea of stew was anything boiled in gallons of water and that's how he served it. When he left, I introduced stews like Mum made.

It takes a while to prepare a good stew, but the end result is well worth it. On a cold winter's night, nothing can beat eating stew with hot crunchy bread, a good bottle of wine and the final touch, a roaring log fire and good friends.

Whenever I see a stew recipe there is one particular story that always comes to mind. It was one of the many times when I was cooking (we were in between cooks) while teaching school to three children, running the office, answering the phone, gardening, being medical officer and dispatch officer – just to mention a few of my jobs. It was just before dinner and I was rushing to throw together a big stew. It was simmering away on the monster wood stove and all I had to do was add some soy sauce for the final flavour, while instructing the children in their school work (they would follow me around the house). The children were sitting at the kitchen table, watching and listening, as I reached down to the shelf, grabbed the soy sauce bottle (or so I thought) and poured a good healthy slug into the pot of stew. When I looked at the plastic bottle I realised that I had just added raspberry syrup to the stew.

Twenty hungry abattoir workers were about to descend on the kitchen – what was I to do? I decided to taste it. It had a strange flavour, but it wasn't unpleasant – it was definitely edible. I quickly fiddled with some spices to counteract the sweetness, adding some ginger, some mixed herbs and a good dose of soy sauce. The final taste wasn't bad. I warned the children not to open their mouths, adding threat of a weekend of school – it was enough to swear them to eternal silence.

'Good stew, Missus. Seems a bit different,' the abbatoir workers remarked as they ate with gusto.

So, I probably created the first sweet stew. I had to smile many years later, when I had a reasonable kitchen and some cookbooks, and I read a recipe that said, 'If you want a different taste to your stew add a few tablespoons of sweet fruit pickles.' Been there, done that.

Below is the recipe *without* the raspberry syrup!

Bullo River Beef Stew

Marinade for beef:

¼ cup light or reduced-salt soy sauce

½ teaspoon grated ginger

1 cup beef stock

1 x 375 ml can beer

Cornflour coating:

1 cup cornflour

½ teaspoon dried mixed herbs

½ teaspoon mustard powder

pinch of ground nutmeg

pinch of salt and pepper

1 tablespoon dried parsley flakes

Marinate beef first: Combine all marinade ingredients in a shallow dish. Add beef and beef shank; mix thoroughly. Cover and refrigerate for 30 minutes or longer if you have time. Drain well.

Coat beef next: Mix all coating ingredients together in a small bowl. Spread drained marinated beef and beef shank out in a single layer on a tray. Sprinkle cornflour mixture over; turn to coat evenly. Reserve any leftover cornflour mixture for thickening the stew.

Stew:

1.5 kg round beef steak, trimmed and cut into 5 cm cubes

1 kg beef shank with bone, cut into 2 cm slices

60 g butter

4 to 6 tablespoons olive oil

6 small onions, quartered

2 cloves garlic, crushed

¼ cup plain flour

3 cups red wine

3 cups beef stock

3 carrots, thickly sliced

250 g mushrooms, if small buttons, leave whole; if larger cups, cut into quarters

1 cup thickly sliced celery

1 cup fresh peas

1 bay leaf

salt and pepper

¼ cup chopped fresh parsley for garnish

To make stew: Place 1 tablespoon each butter and oil in a large heavy-based or non-stick frying pan, over a medium-high heat. When hot, add a third of the beef cubes and brown well. Transfer beef to a plate. Add more butter and oil and repeat process until all beef is browned. Be careful not to put too much beef into the pan at the one time as it will stew and will not brown. Add beef shank last; cook for 10 minutes or until browned.

Put beef and shank into a large, deep casserole or a large, heavy-based pan with a tight-fitting lid. I prefer to cook the stew in the oven as this eliminates checking to see if it is sticking to the bottom of the pan, which, strictly speaking, means it should be called a casserole because stews are cooked on the stovetop!

Add remaining oil to frying pan and gently cook onions and garlic over a medium heat until soft, about 5 minutes. Place on a plate; set aside.

Add flour and any remaining cornflour mixture to frying pan; cook, stirring constantly, for 1 to 2 minutes until golden brown. Do not burn. Add wine and stock; bring to the boil, stirring constantly. Add to beef mixture, along with carrots.

Cover casserole and cook in a moderate oven/180°C for 1 hour. Add onions and garlic, mushrooms, celery, peas and bay leaf. Stir carefully to combine. Cover and cook for a further 30 minutes or until tender. Season to taste with salt and pepper. Serve hot sprinkled with parsley, accompanied with rice or creamy mashed potatoes, Bullo-Style Cabbage (see next recipe) and mashed pumpkin.

SERVES 8 – 10

Bullo-Style Cabbage is reasonably healthy and low in fat and it is wonderful served with Bullo River Beef Stew. Back in the sixties on Bullo, cabbage was one of the few fresh vegetables – apart from potatoes, pumpkin and onions – that we saw. Any food had to be hardy to make the journey to Bullo's kitchen, and only the extremely hardy made it.

The outer layers of leaves were usually unrecognisable, but as you peeled away layer after layer, a cabbage finally appeared – half the size, mind you, but fresh! After weeks of living on dried peas that could be used as ammo for a gun, cabbage tasted like a gift from the gods. I experimented with herbs, spices and other things, finally coming up with the following recipe.

Bullo-Style Cabbage

½ cabbage, finely sliced or shredded

1 chicken stock cube

1 teaspoon grated or ground nutmeg

2 tablespoons butter

Put cabbage in a heavy-based medium-size saucepan with about 1 cm water, just enough to stop the cabbage from sticking and to create a steaming effect. Crumble stock cube over cabbage. Sprinkle with nutmeg and place butter on top.

Cover with a tight-fitting lid and cook on a medium-low heat, until cabbage is tender, shaking pan occasionally while still in contact with heat, about 5-10 minutes. Add more water if necessary to prevent cabbage from burning.

Stir cabbage before placing in a serving bowl and serve sprinkled lightly with a touch of nutmeg.

SERVES 6 – 8

As you can imagine, on a cattle station we are always looking for different ways of serving beef. Bullo River Pot Roast is a favourite recipe that is easy to prepare and even easier to eat!

Bullo River Pot Roast

2 tablespoons olive oil

2 kg topside or fresh silverside or round of beef in a piece

2 tablespoons brown sugar

3 cloves garlic, crushed

3 tablespoons tomato paste

1 chicken stock cube, crumbled

¼ teaspoon dried mixed herbs

1 teaspoon light or reduced-salt soy sauce

4 tablespoons chopped fresh parsley

8 grinds black pepper

60 g butter

3 carrots, cut in chunky pieces

3 parsnips, cut in chunky pieces

8 small onions

6 medium potatoes, peeled and halved

2 stalks celery, cut in 8 cm lengths

1 beef stock cube

2 bay leaves

½ teaspoon grated ginger

1 teaspoon Worcestershire sauce

1 cup red wine

5 cups water

3 tablespoons cornflour

Heat oil in a large heavy-based pan, over a medium-high heat, add beef and brown well on all sides, turning with spoons or eggslices. Do not prick. After 10 minutes, sprinkle 1 tablespoon brown sugar and garlic over beef; brown for a further 5 minutes.

Place beef in a large deep roasting pan with a lid. Spread tomato paste over beef; sprinkle chicken stock cube, mixed herbs, soy sauce, 2 tablespoons parsley and black pepper over the top.

Add butter to pan and cook carrots, parsnips, onions, potatoes and celery on a low heat, stirring occasionally, until golden. Place vegetables on a plate.

Add beef stock cube, bay leaves, remaining brown sugar, ginger, Worcestershire sauce, wine and water to pan. Bring to the boil, stirring to loosen any pan sediment. Pour mixture around beef.

Cook beef in a very hot oven/220°C, for 10 minutes with lid off, reduce temperature to low/120°C, cover and cook slowly for 1½ hours. Place vegetables around beef, cover and cook for a further 1 hour.

Serve beef in thick slices, on a deep serving platter, with vegetables around the beef. Blend cornflour smoothly with ¼ cup water; add to liquid in roasting pan and stir over a medium heat until boiling and thickened. Cook for 1 minute. Serve with beef and vegetables.

SERVES 8

As you have probably noticed by now, desserts and cakes keep creeping into my lists of recipes. The main reason for this is that in the bush one craves sweet food. I am not sure why; maybe the constant hard work has the body looking for an instant energy supply. When the men go without something sweet for a few days, they start raiding my pantry.

I always know when the stockcamp is about thirty kilometres from home. A messenger arrives home in the Toyota carrying a note from Marlee, listing what they need out at the camp. It usually finishes with, 'Send loads of cakes and scones!' This is a favourite stockcamp special.

Apple Cream Cinnamon Cake

125 g unsalted butter
½ cup caster sugar
2 large eggs
1 teaspoon vanilla essence
1 teaspoon bicarbonate of soda
1 cup sour cream
2 cups self-raising flour, sifted
2 cooking apples, peeled, cored and sliced into wedges
½ cup chopped walnuts
2 tablespoons white sugar
2 teaspoons ground cinnamon

Cream together butter and sugar in a mixing bowl until light and fluffy. Add eggs one at a time and beat well after each egg is added. Beat in vanilla.

Mix bicarbonate of soda with sour cream. Fold flour and sour cream mixture alternately into the creamed mixture.

Pour half the cake mixture into a lined and greased 20 cm cake tin. Cover mixture with half the sliced apples. Mix walnuts, sugar and cinnamon together; sprinkle half over the apples. Pour in the remaining cake mixture; cover with the remaining apple slices, arranged in a wheel pattern. Sprinkle with remaining walnut mixture.

Bake in a moderate oven/180°C for 1 hour or until cooked when tested with a fine skewer. Leave cake in tin for 10 minutes before turning out onto a wire cooling rack. A good tip is to firstly turn the cake out onto a plate, so that if the topping moves, you can save it and replace it when the cake is right side up on the cooling rack. Serve on a flat cake plate.

MAKES 8 – 12 SLICES

America always brings to mind food and it was in Maryland that I first learned that exotic food existed. I had been raised as an athlete, on an athlete's diet, from a very early age. I was brought up to think of food as a fuel to make the body perform, so only the best, most healthy and uncomplicated foods were eaten. So after living all my life on grills and baked dinners and Mum's magical sponges, I was plunged into the exotica of Maryland cuisine.

Food was a preoccupation in Maryland – this was something I was not used to. It was discussed at all times and every magazine had pages of recipes and pictures of food. After finishing a three-course breakfast, people would immediately set about discussing what to have for lunch! Little wonder I gained weight.

So, to say that I had fun, in more ways than one, is a complete understatement! There were different eating habits, new food combinations and names – there were traps everywhere and I fell into most of them.

Most sandwich bars did not use butter; they spread the bread with mayonnaise instead. When I braced the counter one day and asked for a banana sandwich, the entire shop fell silent.

'What's shu' want, honey?'

I tried again, 'A banana sandwich,' I slowly articulated.

'Ar don't know dat one. Yu'l have to tell me.' All the shop waited.

'It's just bread, butter and banana.'

'Butter on the bread?'

'Yes!'

'No mayo?'

'No!'

Everyone in the shop watched as she made my apparently strange concoction. All this time I had watched in amazement as the man next to me ordered a marshmallow and chocolate syrup sandwich 'hold the mayo' and no-one batted an eyelid. Yet my banana sandwich with butter brought the shop to a standstill.

'Uuuh hmm, that a strange one,' she said as she handed me my sandwich.

'Not nearly as weird as the one being made up next to you.' I turned and walked out of the shop.

Below is a wonderful American recipe I brought home with me. Maybe if I'd left all these marvellous recipes back in America, I would still be slim!

Pumpkin Chiffon Pie

Gingersnap Pie Crust:

1⅔ cups gingersnap crumbs, about 22 gingersnaps (use gingernuts in Australia)

¼ cup unsalted butter, melted

¼ cup caster sugar

Filling:

4 large egg yolks

1 cup caster sugar

1½ cups pumpkin puree

1 cup milk

½ teaspoon ground ginger

¼ teaspoon ground nutmeg

1 teaspoon ground cinnamon

¼ teaspoon ground cloves

2 tablespoons unsalted butter

3 teaspoons gelatine

¼ cup warm water

4 large egg whites

whipped cream and Maple-Glazed Pecans for decoration

To make Pie Crust: Combine gingersnap crumbs, butter and sugar in a mixing bowl. Mix well. Press mixture over the bottom and sides of a 23 cm pie dish. Chill.

To make Filling: Combine egg yolks, ½ cup sugar, pumpkin puree, milk, spices and butter in the top of a double-boiler. Place over gently bubbling water and stir until thickened to a custard consistency, about 10 minutes. Remove from heat.

In a small bowl, mix gelatine with warm water; add to warm custard and stir well until dissolved. Chill until mixture starts to thicken.

Whisk egg whites in a large, clean polished bowl, until stiff. Add remaining sugar gradually, whisking constantly. Fold into chilled mixture. Pour mixture into pie crust and chill until firm.

Serve pie decorated with whipped cream and Maple-Glazed Pecans.

SERVES 12

Maple-Glazed Pecans

16 pecan halves
¼ cup of maple syrup
2 teaspoons golden syrup

Bake pecan halves in a 160°C oven for 15 minutes; cool.

Combine maple syrup and golden syrup in a small saucepan and place over a medium heat until mixture is a rich caramel-brown.

Working very quickly, stick a toothpick into each pecan and swirl it rapidly in the syrup. Place pecans on an oiled baking tray and allow to cool. The syrup hardens quickly, so work fast.

Arrange the glazed pecans attractively on the Pumpkin Chiffon Pie, or use to decorate other pies and cakes.

As well as bringing home recipes from America, I also took some Australian classics to the States. I planned to make a pavlova for a dinner party as no-one had ever heard of it in Maryland and I went in search of passionfruit in the local supermarket. I asked the man if he had any passionfruit and he thought I was being forward, trying to pick him up!

He really didn't believe it was a fruit. Maryland was a small country town and it seems they didn't have much call for passionfruit. If I wanted passionfruit it was a two-hour drive to the big supermarket in Washington. Passionfruit were in the 'import section', next to the miniature corn from Israel. I spent the next month avoiding the supermarket man.

When I came back to Australia from America my cooking conditions were somewhat different. The kitchen at Bullo didn't even have walls, let alone a shelf to put a cookbook on.

The following recipe brings back memories of an unlined tin shed with a terrifying steel contraption in the corner that I was supposed to use to cook food! I haven't cooked this recipe for such a long time, but the memory of the flavour always lingers in my mind.

Mango Chicken, Bullo-Style

1.5 kg skinless chicken breast fillets

2 tablespoons olive or peanut oil

1 clove garlic, crushed

1 ½ teaspoons grated ginger

1 tablespoon fruit chutney

2 tablespoons butter

finely grated rind and juice of 1 lemon

finely grated rind and juice of 1 lime

2 tablespoons light or reduced-salt soy sauce

¼ cup dry sherry

½ teaspoon sesame oil

2 x 250g cans mangoes with juice

3 tablespoons cornflour

½ cup water

2 mangoes, peeled, stoned and sliced (use frozen if out of season)

Trim chicken and cut into single breasts. Heat oil in a large heavy-based frying pan or sauté pan over a medium-high heat; add chicken in batches and cook until golden, about 2 minutes on each side. As the chicken is browned, set aside on a plate.

Add garlic, ginger, fruit chutney, butter, lemon rind and juice, lime rind and juice, soy sauce, sherry and sesame oil to pan and stir over a low heat until combined. Add mango juice; stir well. Blend cornflour smoothly with water; add to pan mixture and bring to the boil over a medium heat, stirring constantly.

Add fresh and canned mangoes and chicken to sauce in pan; reduce heat to low, cover and simmer for 20 minutes, spooning the sauce over the chicken occasionally, or until chicken is tender.

Serve hot with rice and vegetables.

SERVES 12

The valley is alive with noise and movement. Baby calves and foals, having lost their shaky birth legs, run everywhere with confidence. Experts on life after a few short months, they are full of insatiable curiosity, wanting to know what is behind every blade of grass.

The river sparkles — even though it is brown — washed clean of debris by the torrential rains of January and February, and billabong and creek waters are crystal clear. Although in parts of the river you can see a fallen tree, over 10 metres down, the water is so clear, deep and sparkling you feel you can touch the tree just below the surface. It seems so close, lying in the pristine waters that only isolated wilderness can produce.

April

Hot Cross Buns

~

Bullo Apple Turnovers

~

Lemon-Lime Butter Icing

~

Baked Mince Lamb Steaks

~

Mint Pesto

~

Ginger Prawns in Herb Bread Slices

~

Bullo Orange Wild Duck

~

Marlee's Wild Duck, Created for Franz

~

Eggs, White House-Style

~

Salad of Salmon, Orange and Avocado

~

I t's Easter, time for the Easter bunny – a must, no matter how busy we are. I think Charlie often had more fun than the girls. Back in the late seventies my life on the station was living hell. I suggested that maybe we could skip the Easter egg hunt, the special meals, the chocolate Easter eggs and the hot cross buns. I reasoned that the girls were older and they would understand; we could make it up to them by doing something nice when we made it to town next. Charlie was horrified – miss the egg hunt, the extra drinking time, the hot cross buns? He wouldn't hear of it.

Another time when the girls were very young – around nine, seven and two – and we had just returned from America, I found myself on the station, out in the middle of nowhere, with Easter approaching and I was not prepared. The children had just spent four years living in Maryland and were right up on the festivities of Easter.

I put in some hasty, emergency telegrams to arrange for the mail plane to bring loads of goodies but the north had late rain that week so the mail plane didn't arrive.

What to do? I had three little girls waiting patiently for the Easter bunny to arrive in a few days and hide all the Easter eggs for them to find. They were looking forward to loads of chocolates and hot cross buns for breakfast and all of this excitement and anticipation was fired up by the biggest child of them all – Charlie.

Opposite: Hot Cross Buns (recipe page 74). Following pages: Bullo Orange Wild Duck (recipe page 82) and Marlee's Wild Duck, Created for Franz (recipe page 83).

How could I explain that Easter wasn't the same in Australia? And how could I explain what the non-arrival of the mail plane had to do with the Easter bunny coming? I just couldn't. I had to create an Easter with a difference, outback Bullo-style.

We had no eggs – they were in the order on the mail plane – but we did have young coconut trees growing and the small (or seed) coconuts were just about the size of a hen egg, so they became our Easter eggs. I painted them all colours of the rainbow and they looked just the part. In fact they were better – the children could sit on them, throw them, fall on top of them and there wasn't a dent or a child screaming that their Easter egg was broken. I melted cooking chocolate and cut out some weird and wonderful shapes that were supposed to be rabbits.

Charlie and the girls had a wonderful egg hunt and then, hot and sweaty, they sat down to eat the funny chocolate figures, complaining about the quality of the chocolate.

I made my first hot cross buns; they were mediocre, but disappeared the moment they hit the plate. I had no idea how to get the cross, so when they were cooked I cut a cross into the brown tops and the white bread showed through.

It was our first Easter on Bullo, and I suppose it is an Easter that I will always remember.

A few years ago we were in the same predicament – late rains, no mail plane and no hot cross buns.

So I made my second lot of hot cross buns, twenty-five years after the first batch. They were a little different – this time I knew how to get the cross on the buns and I also added a professional touch by glazing them. When Marlee came in from grading the road, she wanted to know how I got fresh hot cross buns from the shop!

Opposite: Mango Chicken, Bullo-Style (recipe page 66) served with rice and snowpeas.

Hot Cross Buns

30 g fresh compressed yeast
¼ cup caster sugar
4 cups plain flour
1½ cups lukewarm milk
1 teaspoon salt
½ teaspoon ground mixed spice
½ teaspoon ground cinnamon
60 g butter
1 egg, beaten
¾ cup sultanas

Cream (mix) yeast with 1 teaspoon each of the sugar and the flour in a small mixing bowl until it turns to a liquid. Add lukewarm milk; mix well. Cover and stand in a warm place for 15 minutes or until the mixture looks frothy.

Sift flour, salt, sugar and spices into a large mixing bowl. Add butter and rub in with the fingertips and thumbs. Add egg, sultanas and yeast mixture; beat well with a wooden spoon. Cover bowl with clear plastic wrap and a tea towel and stand in a warm place for 40 minutes or until dough doubles in bulk.

Punch dough down; turn onto a floured surface and knead well until dough is smooth to touch and is elastic (springs back when you push it).

Cut dough into 3 equal pieces, then divide each piece into 4 or 5 to make 12 or 15 buns. Knead each piece of dough into a round shape. Put buns in a lightly greased 18 x 28 cm shallow cake tin. Cover and stand in a warm place for a further 15 minutes or until buns have risen.

To make the cross: Sift ½ cup plain flour into a small bowl; mix to a paste with ⅓ cup water. Put mixture into a small piping bag or a plastic bag with a small hole cut in the corner. Pipe a cross of mixture on each risen bun.

Bake buns in a hot oven/200°C for 20 minutes or until cooked and browned. Remove from oven; immediately brush with a glaze made by dissolving 1 tablespoon sugar and 1 teaspoon gelatine in 1 tablespoon of hot water. Remove buns from tin and cool on a wire cooling rack.

MAKES 12 – 15

April is usually the start of the new season, time to start mustering. The change in the weather is noticeable. The temperature moves down into the low thirties, which is quite refreshing. The humidity is gone and you suddenly have more energy. A very hot day creeps into the week now and then but most of the time the weather is quite pleasant.

The paddocks start to dry out, making travel off the road, for the first time in four months, possible. It is time to assess what the rainy season has brought us.

The obvious bonuses are seen close by. The cattle are rolling fat — well, what we in the north call 'rolling fat'. To the southern cattle people it would be called 'average condition', but to us it is rolling fat.

The hay crop is tall and green, waving in the morning breeze, waiting to be harvested. The cattle spend the days trying to break into the paddocks to save us the trouble of harvesting it ourselves.

We have to venture further afield to check fences which have been inaccessible during the flooding of the lower paddocks. But the biggest concern is how the road fared during the torrential rains of the past months.

We cut down slightly on our salt intake, bringing it back to a level that is still above what is considered normal. There is a lot of sweaty work to be done in April and May to get the station moving for the new season. Salt intake will be back to normal levels in about June.

Every day we seem to be going off in a different direction, checking off the long list of sites we must visit.

Sandwiches feature prominently in April and all through the mustering season. When Marlee goes out to check the road, it is usually an all-day trip. First she has to drive 150 kilometres just to get to the front gate and back, but it isn't a straight drive. Fallen trees have to be moved off the road, creeks that have silted up need to be cleared. Flash flood creeks (created when a wall of water moves down the creek leaving hardly any water after it passes) usually wash the entire road about seven metres downstream. This means that you are often faced with a gaping great big hole instead of a road crossing the creek.

Sometimes, after a really bad wet season, it can take two days to reach the front gate. Marlee is driving the grader, instead of a normal vehicle, so of course the going is slow.

Every morning the kitchen resembles a sandwich shop at peak hour, with orders being shouted back and forth, eskies getting packed and water containers filled to the top with ice then topped up with water.

Biscuits, good solid travelling cakes and slices are cooked in a never-ending supply and bread is brought into the station by the box, on a regular basis. The days of making bread are gone, there is just no spare time to make it. With the introduction of the freezer, life became easier, especially in the bread department. Every now and then we make a few loaves, just to have the smell of freshly baked bread wafting around your nostrils. A few deep breaths of freshly baked bread can change your whole outlook on the day.

An endless supply of packed meals move out of the kitchen in the first month of starting the mustering season. When you are the cook it is a nightmare, because you are virtually putting together three meals for all the workers in the few short hours before breakfast.

By 7.00 am they are all gone and there is a welcome silence, but the kitchen looks like a bomb has just been dropped in it. Even though there are no meals to speak of for the rest of the day, you are 'flat to the boards' cooking, making what is needed for the next day. Grilling steak, roasting meat for sandwiches, making pies, pizza, cake, biscuits, slice and drink mixtures – the list goes on.

Food still tends to be on the salt side – to counteract the constant sweating and loss of body fluids – so we use sardines, tuna and anchovies in most of the savoury fillings, supplemented with steak and roasts.

Many a time, with a new cook, I have walked into the kitchen to find her reading a magazine, thinking that there is nothing to cook because everyone is away for the day. When I mention that all the food for ten people has to be cooked, packed and ready to leave at 5.30 the next morning, she will quickly put down the magazine and get to work.

Food high in energy is needed for people doing hard physical work. Steak, pies and pastry (all high in fat content) are needed, along with sweet snacks to keep the energy levels up.

I started making Apple Turnovers way back in the sixties in America. I was browsing in the frozen cake section of the supermarket one day and I saw a packet of apple turnovers. I was fascinated to read that everything, including the icing, was in the box – I had to try them.

So that was how I came to make my first apple turnovers and over thirty years later they are still high on the list of favourites at Bullo. Marlee and I have improved on the flavour of the first frozen version made in the USA!

Bullo Apple Turnovers

8 large green cooking apples

¾ cup light brown sugar

2 teaspoons ground cinnamon

1 teaspoon ground nutmeg

6 cloves

grated rind and juice of 1 lemon

40 g butter

4 sheets frozen puff pastry (1 sheet makes 4 turnovers)

½ cup sultanas

Lemon-Lime Butter Icing (see recipe following)

Slice apples and leave skin on; remove core. Place in a large heavy-based pan; add water, enough to cover by 2 cm. Add ½ cup sugar, cinnamon, nutmeg, cloves, lemon rind and juice; also toss in the rest of the lemon for the cooking.

Boil, uncovered, until apples are soft and liquid has reduced. Apples should be dark from the spices. Add butter and let melt over the apples. Drain off any excess liquid; remove cloves and lemon. Cool until cold.

Defrost pastry according to pack instructions. Cut one sheet of pastry into quarters. Put a tablespoon of apple mixture in the centre of each square; add 2 teaspoons sultanas and sprinkle with 1 teaspoon of remaining brown sugar.

Fold pastry over to opposite corner to form a triangle. Seal by pressing with a fork along the 2 sides. Press in about 1.5 cm to make a nice pattern. Place on a baking tray and put 2 holes in the top of each turnover.

Complete all turnovers as directed above. Bake in a very hot oven/250°C, for 20 minutes or until golden brown.

Cool turnovers on a wire cooling rack. While turnovers are still slightly warm, top with the Lemon-Lime Butter Icing and let it melt over the pastry.

SERVES 8

Lemon-Lime Butter Icing

¾ x 500 g packet icing sugar
40 g unsalted butter
juice and rind of 1 lemon
juice and rind of 1 lime
boiling water to mix

Sift icing sugar into a mixing bowl. Add lemon rind and lime rind. Make a well (hollow) in the middle and add the butter, then some boiling water, a little at a time, on top of the butter, mixing as you go. Add the lemon juice and lime juice and mix well. Keep adding boiling water, mixing well, until the icing is a spreading consistency.

Top Bullo Apple Turnovers with Lemon-Lime Butter Icing as directed.

Although the workers need foods high in fat, I'm constantly searching for tasty recipes that are low in fat. Sometimes we adapt existing recipes.

In the next two recipes I have tried to replace deep frying with baking in the oven and I have added an interesting sauce to replace the flavour of deep frying. With the second recipe I have experimented with baked herb bread slices to replace the very fattening pastry.

Baked Mince Lamb Steaks

1 kg finely minced 'Trim' lamb

2 onions, finely chopped

6 spring onions / shallots, finely chopped

3 cloves garlic, crushed

2 eggs, beaten

2 tablespoons finely chopped fresh parsley

plain flour for dipping

olive oil spray for baking

Coating:

2 cups fresh breadcrumbs

90 g flaked almonds, toasted and lightly crushed

1 teaspoon ground cumin

⅓ cup chopped fresh mint

1 tablespoon chopped fresh parsley

12 grinds black pepper

Combine the lamb, onions, spring onions, garlic, eggs and parsley in a mixing bowl. Mix well. Press mixture level and divide into 8 equal portions.

With clean, cold wet hands, shape each portion of the mixture to resemble a small steak, about 1 cm thick, dipping in flour, when necessary, to bind together.

To make Coating: Mix all ingredients together in a bowl. Place coating on a sheet of greaseproof paper.

Place steaks in coating; turn to coat well and press mixture on to make it stick.

Place steaks in a single layer in a lightly oiled shallow baking dish; spray a little olive oil over each steak. Bake in a moderate oven/180°C for 30 minutes or until golden brown and cooked.

Serve lamb steaks with Mint Pesto Sauce or fat-free mint jelly.

Serves 8

Mint Pesto

4 cloves garlic, halved

1 cup fresh mint leaves

½ cup fresh parsley leaves

⅓ cup walnut halves

½ teaspoon cracked black peppercorns

½ cup virgin olive oil

mint sauce, optional

Place garlic, mint, parsley, walnuts and peppercorns into a food processor and whiz until just chopped. With the machine still running, pour in the oil in a thin stream until combined.

If too thick, add some mint sauce until sauce is the consistency of poring sauce. Serve with Baked Mince Lamb Steaks or over freshly cooked spaghetti.

Ginger Prawns in Herb Bread Slices

1 kg green king prawns, shelled and deveined

30 g butter

2 spring onions/shallots, chopped

1 red capsicum, thinly sliced

2 tablespoons grated ginger

2 tablespoons dry white wine

2 tablespoons fresh lemon juice

1 teaspoon French mustard

1 teaspoon brown sugar

2 tablespoons plain flour

¼ cup cream

¾ cup milk

½ cup coarsely chopped fresh parsley

Bread Slices:

8 thick slices fresh white bread

⅓ cup French mustard

2 tablespoons finely chopped fresh parsley

1 tablespoon grated ginger

2 cloves garlic, crushed

⅓ cup freshly grated parmesan cheese

Cut prawns into 1 cm pieces. Heat 2 teaspoons butter in a non-stick frying pan, add prawns and cook over a medium heat, stirring frequently, until cooked and colour changes to an orange-red. Remove from heat.

Heat remaining butter in a saucepan over a low heat; add spring onions, capsicum, ginger and wine. Cook, stirring occasionally, for about 4 minutes or until capsicum is soft.

Add lemon juice, mustard, sugar and flour; stir over a medium heat for 2 minutes. Remove from heat; gradually stir in cream and milk. Stir over a medium heat until mixture boils and thickens, reduce heat and simmer for 1 minute.

Stir the prawns and parsley into the sauce; keep warm.

To make Bread Slices: Cut crusts off bread and roll flat with a rolling pin. Spread both sides of each slice with mustard. Sprinkle one side only of each slice with parsley, ginger, garlic and parmesan cheese, dividing equally.

Grill this side under the grill until golden and nicely cooked. Grill one side only.

Make 4 sandwiches out of the 8 bread slices, with the soft ungrilled sides together, filled evenly with the ginger prawns. Serve immediately with a green salad.

SERVES 4

Each day allows us to move further afield into areas and paddocks that were under water during the first months of the year. In some areas you could only get to the fences by swimming, but that is out of the question. When the river breaks its banks and floods the paddocks, it is not unusual to see a saltwater crocodile cruising casually through the trees a few kilometres into a paddock, floating along in the flood waters, surveying the new territory.

When the river, and, more importantly, the crocs, go back to within the river banks and the paddocks dry out, we venture out to see if our fences are still there or if they have been washed a few kilometres downstream. Everything has to be repaired before the cattle go back to the area.

Marlee is first to venture out onto the road – the assessment of the road is really the first step in getting the station moving. It is important to know how many rock slides have covered the road, especially in the areas where it winds up through cliffs and hills for many kilometres.

Cascading water from heavy downpours can pound it into oblivion, requiring heavy work to bring it back to looking like a road again. Once we know how much work is required and what machines are needed, then other jobs like fence repairs, machinery maintenance and water supply to the outer paddocks can be planned.

Meanwhile, back in the kitchen, sandwiches, cakes and more sandwiches are being made.

April brings us Marlee's birthday. One year, Franz shot a wild duck for her birthday, but Marlee had to cook it. We had always used our Bullo Orange Wild Duck, which over the years Marlee had perfected to our taste.

When Marlee cooked this superb dish for Franz the first time, he said, in his typical, straightforward manner, 'I do not like that.'

Marlee was horrified, but never to be beaten she created a special duck recipe just for Franz. Both recipes follow.

Bullo Orange Wild Duck

This recipe is also suitable for domestic duck.

2 kg duck, plucked and dressed

60 g butter, melted

2 tablespoons light or reduced-salt soy sauce

freshly ground black pepper

Sauce:

1 orange

2 teaspoons cornflour

1 tablespoon honey

2 teaspoons vinegar

2 cups chicken stock

¼ cup lemon juice

¼ cup Grand Marnier

¼ cup dry red wine

pepper to taste

1 clove garlic, crushed

1 teaspoon grated ginger

½ onion, thinly sliced

You may stuff the duck with a stuffing of your choice or use the stuffing recipe in the December recipes.

Brush duck with melted butter and soy sauce. Sprinkle with freshly ground black pepper. Lightly grease a roasting pan with olive oil. Place the duck on a rack in the prepared pan and roast in a moderate oven/180°C for 1 hour, basting frequently with the pan juices. If cooking wild duck you will need to cover the breast with bacon rashers to stop the meat drying out.

To make Sauce: Peel rind from the orange with a vegetable peeler; cut into thin julienne strips. Place orange rind into a small pan of boiling water and boil for 3 minutes; drain. Squeeze juice from orange and reserve ½ cup juice. Blend cornflour smoothly with orange juice in a saucepan. Add the remaining sauce ingredients; bring to the boil stirring constantly, then simmer until thickened, about 2 minutes.

Drain off any excess fat from the duck. Baste duck with orange sauce and roast for a further 50 minutes, basting frequently, until duck is well cooked and nicely glazed.

Serve hot with new potatoes tossed in chopped parsley and butter and freshly cooked vegetables.

SERVES 4

Marlee's Wild Duck, Created for Franz

Marinade:

1/3 cup extra virgin olive oil

10 large cloves garlic, peeled

1 cup light or reduced-salt soy sauce

2 cups red wine

1 cup cranberry sauce

grated rind and juice of 1 orange

pepper to taste

Duck:

4 wild ducks, plucked and dressed

4 rashers bacon

To make Marinade: Combine all ingredients in a bowl and stir well.

Place ducks in a large shallow dish. Pour marinade over; turn ducks to coat well. Cover with clear plastic wrap and marinate the ducks overnight in the refrigerator.

Put ducks and marinade into a roasting pan. Cook in a hot oven/200°C for 30 minutes to brown the ducks. Cut the bacon rashers in half and lay on top of each duck. Reduce the oven temperature to 150°C and cook gently for 1–1½ hours, depending on size of the ducks, spooning liquid over the ducks regularly during roasting. You will end up with a rich sauce that does not need thickening.

To make the perfect meal, Franz likes plain rice, green salad and a good red wine served with the duck.

Serves 4

The funniest duck story I remember had to be when Charlie was entertaining an old navy friend from New York. They were in the war together and had stayed friends over the years. He was out visiting the Far East and extended his trip to visit Charlie at Bullo.

What a culture shock. He was now somewhere near the top in the navy and expected the strict protocol of the service. Charlie had left that all behind twenty years before and took delight in shocking his friend with the harsh outback reality.

The shock treatment started at Darwin airport. Joe stepped out of America's latest (circa 1976) state-of-the-art fighter plane, having just had a VIP sightseeing tour.

Charlie chugged up in our little yellow fabric Super Cub, parked it next to the magnificent shiny machine and calmly said, 'So, are you ready to go? Hope you don't have much luggage – I had to get some last-minute things for Sara, so there's not much room in the luggage compartment.'

Apparently Joe almost refused to get in the plane – she looked so flimsy next to the jet fighter – but Charlie shamed him into it. His staff and pilots stood open-mouthed as Charlie stuffed their superior officer into the little plane and then piled the luggage on top of him, while complaining that there was too much. Charlie waved a cheery goodbye as the little plane struggled into the air and slowly – for what must have seemed an eternity to a jet pilot – disappeared out of sight.

In a few minutes flat Joe had gone from flying in a supersonic jet fighter to a two-hour plus flight in an aircraft made of cloth, with a speed that depended on whether the plane was going with the wind or against it.

Charlie wanted to serve duck for dinner, so in preparation for this great visit Marlee was dispatched as the hunter with the instruction to collect a duck per person. It was late into the afternoon and Marlee was tired, but she still had one more duck to go. She watched as the sun slipped behind the hills, wondering if she would get the quota demanded by her father. Finally, a duck circled. Marlee was alert, the shot rang out and the duck fell to the ground in the reeds along the edge of the billabong. Marlee rushed to the spot to retrieve it, happy she could now go home.

When she touched the duck, it jumped up, started running around and flapping its wings, but not flying. Marlee thought she had wounded it, so she tried to catch it. They went up the billabong, down the billabong, around the billabong and crisscrossed it too many times to count.

Exhausted, Marlee slumped down on the ground and watched through tears of frustration as the stupid duck finally got airborne and flew away. She was certain she had hit it with a clean shot, but no duck could do all that after being shot, she reasoned, or even if it was just slightly wounded. 'Oh well,' she thought, 'it looks like I am one duck short.'

Wearily she pulled herself up and started walking back to her camp site and the other ducks.

She stopped short when she came to a dead duck lying on the edge of the reeds. It was the duck she had shot! She had not been chasing the duck she had shot. Instead, it had been a young duck that was hiding in the reeds. When the dead duck fell next to it and Marlee appeared, it scared the living daylights out of the poor thing and off it took, running. It was so young that it was still in its flying program. A half hour with Marlee advanced its flying program by a few weeks.

The ducks were served for dinner the next night and it took all day to prepare for Charlie's great banquet. The table did look a picture, laid with all the best silver and crystal. I was very proud of our effort and the girls toiled with me all day to create the dinner.

When we finally sat down, the large platter of ducks was passed around and we had one whole duck each. Our guest was amazed – he asked me did I realise how much money was sitting on the table?

I assumed he was referring to the silver and crystal and said I had no idea, but some of the silver was very old, as was some of the crystal.

'No,' he said. He wasn't talking about that – he meant the value of the ducks! In New York in the seventies you would get on a 'duck hunting bus' that would take you to Maryland on Friday night, then hunt ducks on Saturday and Sunday mornings and drive back to New York on Sunday night in time to be at the office on Monday. The cost was two thousand dollars and the hunting limit was one duck per person, per day, making each wild duck worth one thousand dollars.

You would then host a dinner party for as many people as possible. Each guest received a tiny piece of duck to savour, while listening to your hunting tales and the cost of the mouthful they were about to swallow. No wonder he was amazed when he was served the whole duck!

In 1969 I had breakfast in the White House in Washington, with the First Lady ... and about three hundred other women. Senators' wives could invite a friend along to these breakfasts and I played tennis with the Maryland senator and his wife, so that's how I ended up having breakfast at the White House.

We were served an amazing concoction that was called scrambled eggs, but the only connection with the scrambled eggs that I knew was the word eggs. Like all of the cooking in America this was very rich, but delicious. I commented how delicious it was, and before I knew it I was given the recipe. I was told that this was, indeed, a rare event, but 'my friend the Senator' had a lot of pull in Washington.

Eggs, White House-Style

Breakfast with the First Lady.

Basic Cream Sauce:

1 tablespoon plain flour

1 tablespoon butter

1 cup hot milk

heavy dash of Worcestershire sauce

salt and black pepper

Hollandaise Sauce in a blender (no cooking):

3 egg yolks

1 tablespoon fresh lemon juice

dash of cayenne pepper

125 g butter

To make Basic Cream Sauce: Place butter and flour in the top of a double-boiler, over gently boiling water, over low heat; stir constantly for about 2 minutes. Then add hot milk gradually, stirring all the time.

Increase the heat until the water in the boiler is very hot and cook for 10 minutes, stirring often. Season to taste with Worcestershire sauce, salt and pepper.

If you want a thicker sauce, increase the flour to 3 tablespoons and the butter to 2 tablespoons.

To make Hollandaise Sauce: Place egg yolks in a blender with lemon juice and cayenne pepper. Cover. Quickly turn blender on then off.

Eggs:

6 large eggs

6 large tomatoes, sliced into 3 thick slices

4 tablespoons chopped fresh parsley

2 cloves garlic, crushed

6 rashers bacon, finely chopped and fried until crisp

½ cup freshly grated parmesan cheese

4-6 thick slices French bread

chopped fresh parsley for garnish

Heat butter to almost boiling. Turn blender onto high speed, and slowly pour the butter into mixture. Blend until thick and fluffy, about 30 seconds.

Place sauce over warm, not hot water until serving time.

To make eggs: Break eggs into a bowl, beat lightly. Fill a cup ¾ full with egg, add ¼ of Basic Cream Sauce. Use up the rest of the eggs, using this ¾ to ¼ mixture of the eggs and Basic Cream Sauce.

Scramble this mixture in a buttered frying pan to only a soft consistency; don't overcook. Set aside, keep warm.

Cook the tomatoes in a second buttered frying pan, until just softened but still intact. Place in a grill pan and top with the mixture of parsley, garlic and bacon. Sprinkle each tomato slice with 2 teaspoons of parmesan cheese and cook under the grill until cheese is bubbling. Place on individual plates, keep warm.

Toast the French bread and place in grill pan.

Spoon scrambled eggs onto toast then top with a mixture of 2 parts Hollandaise Sauce and 1 part Basic Cream Sauce. Put under the grill until hot and bubbly.

Serve immediately with tomatoes and garnish with chopped parsley.

SERVES 4 – 6

I had many interesting experiences with food while living in America. A group of ladies arrived on my doorstep unannounced one morning, not long after the 'crab affair' dinner. I know they just wanted to meet this strange creature from that place called Australia.

I had no cake in the house and this was a major disaster for any American household. I racked my brain for something that I could serve with their coffee.

I made toast, spread it thinly with Vegemite, cut into fingers, and then sprinkled lightly with chopped parsley. Well, this brought an amazing response from the ladies and they all wanted to know how I made it.

When I told them that it came in a jar, they were a little deflated and didn't hold me in as much awe, but they all still had to have some.

For the next year or so Mum had to send me regular shipments of Vegemite, until one day I stumbled across it in the 'import section' of the Washington supermarket. From then on I just directed the inquiries for Vegemite to Washington.

Lamingtons were another outright winner and always made an impression. Although I was deep in exotic food country my Australian cuisine was creating quite a stir.

We serve foods differently to the Americans, as I found out when we were travelling to New York. We had left Maryland early to avoid the morning traffic and so when we were through the bottle-neck area we stopped for breakfast. I ordered two boiled eggs, medium soft. I was presented with a soup bowl with mashed-up eggs in it with melted butter over the top with pepper and salt. When I said I wanted boiled eggs, I was told, 'That's what ya got!'

I said, 'No, I wanted them in their shells.'

Well, I was finally served two eggs rolling around on a dinner plate. They had never heard of egg cups. The whole restaurant watched as I ate the egg out of the shell with a spoon.

Opposite: Afternoon tea on the homestead verandah. Bullo Banana Cake (recipe page 164) with Hazelnut Mock Cream (recipe page 165), Bullo River Scones (recipe page 100) with jam and cream, and Apple Cream Cinnamon Cake (recipe page 62). Following page: Leg of Lamb with Herb Crust (recipe page 123) served with baked vegetables.

The following recipe is a favourite when a hot day creeps back into our working week.

Salad of Salmon, Orange and Avocado

This salad uses raw fish, Japanese-style, and is light and delicious. If preferred, grill the salmon and flake into chunky pieces, then cool and use as recipe directs.

500 g fresh salmon fillets

2 avocados

2 oranges

4 cups mixed salad greens

6 spring onions/shallots, thinly sliced diagonally

½ cup fresh orange juice

1 tablespoon fresh coriander leaves

1 tablespoon chopped fresh parsley

Dressing:

2 teaspoons grated orange rind

1 teaspoon grated lemon rind

2 cloves garlic, crushed

3 tablespoons olive oil

3 tablespoons red wine vinegar

salt and black pepper to taste

1 teaspoon cumin seeds, roasted

Skin salmon; cut into slices 0.5 cm thick and about 5 cm long. Check there are no bones. Refrigerate until required.

Halve, stone and peel avocados; slice into long wedges.

Peel oranges and remove all skin, including pith, using a serrated knife. Cut into segments; remove pips.

Wash salad greens; pat dry in a clean tea towel.

To make dressing: In a salad bowl, whisk orange and lemon rind, garlic, olive oil, vinegar, salt, pepper and cumin seeds together, until mixture thickens slightly.

Add salad greens to dressing and toss gently. Arrange salmon, avocados, orange segments and spring onions on top of salad greens; pour orange juice over the salad. Sprinkle coriander and parsley over the top. Serve immediately.

SERVES 4

May

Sara's Sunday Quick Spaghetti Lunch

~

Baked Bullo Barra

~

Sweet-and-Sour Sauce

~

Baked Chinese Barra in Foil

~

Bullo River Scones

~

Oxtail Stew

~

Garlic Prawns

~

My Mum's Lemon Dumplings

~

Bullo Dream Layered Cake

~

During May the phone rings endlessly with people wanting jobs, so the phone interviews start.

Usually, with the stockmen, the less they say, the more they can do. With the women, it's hard to tell. In April and May we are well into the endless task of finding a new cook and this situation doesn't improve with time. Each year we keep our fingers crossed hoping a miracle will happen — we are still waiting. In the meantime, Marlee and I take turns in cooking, if and when I'm home (which is not very often). So in recent years the job has fallen on Marlee's head most of the time. It is not unusual for her to work all day on the bulldozer, grader or horse and then rush into the kitchen to whip up a gourmet meal in minutes.

The more we have to cook ourselves, the more desperate we are to find a cook. In the meantime I usually cook for Marlee on Sundays. She sits back, puts her tired feet on the stone coffee table in front of TV and I serve my Sunday special.

We have one big meal mid-afternoon, then something very light for dinner. If we are really good we have fruit and go to bed, before we weaken.

Sara's Sunday Quick Spaghetti Lunch

1 tablespoon olive oil

6 spring onions/shallots

6 cloves garlic, crushed

1 teaspoon grated ginger

10 medium mushrooms, sliced

4 large tomatoes, chopped

1 cup tomato juice

1 teaspoon light or reduced-salt soy sauce

1 teaspoon Worcestershire sauce

1 cup coarsely chopped fresh parsley

200 g spaghetti

½ – ¾ cup freshly grated parmesan cheese

Heat a heavy-based frying pan on a medium heat; add oil and gently cook spring onions, garlic and ginger for 1 minute, until about half cooked. Add mushrooms and tomatoes and cook for a minute to so, stirring frequently.

Add tomato juice, soy sauce and Worcestershire sauce; heat through just until bubbling hot. Add ¼ cup parsley; stir well.

Meanwhile, cook the spaghetti in a large pan, in lots of boiling salted water, until tender, about 10 minutes. When cooked, drain well.

Place spaghetti in individual pasta bowls, in layers with half the parmesan cheese and parsley sprinkled between each layer, dividing equally.

Spoon the sauce evenly over the layered spaghetti and top with the remaining parmesan cheese and lots of parsley. Serve with fresh crunchy bread (diet-style), garlic bread (non-diet style!) or Melba toast.

SERVES 2

I thought I had told all the 'cook' stories in the other books, but, of course, as the cooks keep turning up, so do the stories.

The first cook of the season arrived – or should I say 'the person we hired, because she said she could cook'. When a new cook arrives, everyone waits anxiously. Franz is particularly fussy and likes Marlee or me to cook, but he knows that this cannot be on a regular basis.

When the first meal is placed on the table we know. Marlee and I have been cooking for so long, we can tell just by looking at the kitchen a few hours after the cook arrives, whether we need to make another phone call.

Number one didn't last long – she was a vegetarian who wouldn't touch meat. Why would you apply for a job cooking on a cattle station if you won't touch meat? You have to be touched in the head!

Number two was another vegetarian! No, sorry, this one was a vegan. This was many years ago and being a 'vegan' had just become popular, but being out in the bush, we had not caught up with the latest fad.

I thought she had said virgin, not vegan! Well, I thought that was a strange remark to tell your prospective boss, but what the hell, she would have to be a bit loopy to survive the mob we had working there at the time, so I told her the job was hers. The first thing she did when she arrived was to hand me a long list of the food she needed to eat.

I looked down the list and said, 'Good heavens, what's wrong with you? Have you got anything that's contagious?'

She made an impatient expression and replied, 'No, I told you over the phone I am a vegan.'

Marlee, who was listening to the conversation, cracked up and ran from the kitchen, screaming with laughter. I tried in vain to keep a straight face, but failed miserably. I excused myself and quickly followed Marlee into the bedroom, where we rolled around on the bed for a good ten minutes, in fits of uncontrollable laughter. When we were sure we could control ourselves, we put on a serious face and returned to our now very impatient, irate vegan, who was tapping the list on her hand.

Without looking at Marlee, I seriously informed her that she would be cooking meat, three times a day. She was horrified. I have no idea what she thought she was going to cook on a cattle station, but I didn't go into it – I had glanced at Marlee and once more I made a hasty retreat.

By the time I returned I was told that the vegan had decided to leave, but wanted to know if I could get the list of food requirements in for her until she left. She didn't seem to understand that the next food order would come in on the same plane she left on. I didn't try to explain the system of living 1200 kilometres from the nearest supermarket. The vegan departed after a few days of cooking unbelievable messes.

Marlee and I took turns cooking alternate nights. The first night after the vegan had departed Franz and the entire stockcamp were seated and waiting for dinner a full thirty minutes before Marlee was ready, so keen were they to taste a decent meal.

Franz had caught a massive barra on which Marlee worked her magic. She didn't disappoint them – they all staggered away from the table moaning and sighing with delight.

Baked Bullo Barra

1 whole Bullo barramundi, but any barra, salmon or snapper will do, gutted, cleaned and sealed

1 egg white

1 tablespoon dry sherry or dry white wine

½ teaspoon salt

pinch of black pepper

1 tablespoon water

¼ cup cornflour

extra ½ cup cornflour, for coating fish

½ cup peanut oil

thinly sliced spring onions/shallots for garnish

Slash barramundi diagonally, on both sides, 3 or 4 times.

In a small bowl, mix egg white with sherry, salt, pepper, water and cornflour. Using a brush, coat fish well with the mixture on both sides. Sprinkle fish all over with extra cornflour.

Heat oil in a wok. Holding fish firmly by the tail over the wok, spoon hot oil over the slashes to open them up.

Transfer oil to a large baking dish, adding more oil if necessary, and fry the fish on both sides, turning once, on the stovetop, over a medium-high heat. Fry the fish until crispy.

Drain off remaining oil and bake fish in a moderate oven/180°C until cooked through, about 20–30 minutes. Serve with Sweet-and-Sour Sauce.

SERVES 4 – 8, DEPENDING ON SIZE OF FISH!

Sweet-and-Sour Sauce

3 tablespoons peanut oil

½ onion, cut in wedges

½ carrot, cut in julienne stirps

2 dried Chinese mushrooms, soaked in boiling water for 30 minutes

1 x 227 g can drained and sliced bamboo shoots, cut in julienne strips

½ each red and green capsicum, thinly sliced

4 spring onions/shallots, cut in 5 cm lengths

1 piece fresh ginger, about 2 cm square, cut in julienne strips

5 tablespoons honey

4 tablespoons cider vinegar

4 tablespoons orange juice

3 tablespoons tomato sauce

1 tablespoon soy sauce

1 chicken stock cube, crumbled

1 teaspoon cornflour blended smoothly with 1 tablespoon water

1 tablespoon snipped fresh chives

1 tablespoon chopped fresh parsley

Heat 1 tablespoon oil in the wok and stir-fry all the prepared vegetables until only lightly cooked or tender-crisp, about 2 minutes. Remove from wok.

Heat remaining oil in wok, add all the remaining sauce ingredients and bring to the boil, stirring constantly. Simmer for 2 minutes.

Add vegetables and simmer a further 2 minutes before serving.

Place fish on a large warm serving platter, pour the sauce over and garnish with thinly sliced spring onions. Serve with rice and vegetables or salad.

Once, when we had guests, Franz brought home a barra that was so big it couldn't fit in the oven. Marlee decided to cook it in a steel railway sleeper, in our large barbecue (two half 44-gallon drums welded together end to end). The railway sleeper fitted nicely into the coals in the drum barbecue and the fish, wrapped in foil, fitted snugly into the indent in the railway sleeper. It cooked perfectly in the heat of the sleeper, protected from the coals by the steel. It was delicious!

If you feel creative and have some spare time, try the Baked Bullo Barra with Sweet-and-Sour Sauce. If you don't have the time, but still want to present something just a little bit different, try the following.

Baked Chinese Barra in Foil

1 whole barramundi or salmon or snapper, gutted, cleaned and sealed – size depends on how many you are feeding

⅓ cup light or reduced-salt soy sauce

2 lemons, finely grated rind and juice of 1; the other thinly sliced

¼ cup grated ginger

3 cloves garlic, crushed

⅔ cup roughly chopped fresh parsley

6 spring onions/shallots, thinly sliced

Lay a sheet of thick aluminium foil in the bottom of a large baking dish; brush foil with peanut oil.

Put whole fish on top of foil, rub both sides of it generously with soy sauce and lemon juice. Inside the fish cavity lay the sliced lemon and sprinkle with 1 teaspoon soy sauce and 1 teaspoon lemon juice. Sprinkle ginger, garlic, parsley, spring onions and lemon rind on top of the fish.

Fold the foil up and over the fish to make a sealed package. If foil is not wide enough, put another sheet over the top of the fish and overlap with the bottom sheet of foil. We want to keep the juices in!

Bake in a moderate oven/180°C until tender, about 30–45 minutes depending on size. Check a few times during cooking and spoon juices over the fish each time. Leave foil off the top of the fish for the last 5 minutes to allow the top to go crunchy.

Serve barramundi on a large warm serving platter with the sliced lemon from inside arranged on the top of the fish; pour the juices over and sprinkle with chopped parsley. Serve with new potatoes or rice and salad.

SERVES 4 – 8, DEPENDING ON SIZE OF FISH!

I am the official scone maker on Bullo and I'm sure I could be in the *Guinness Book of Records* for the thousands of trays of scones I have made over the last thirty years.

Good scones are a quick, easy standby for when you have no time. I have made a batch of scones while a plane was circling to land. By the time they had landed and walked into the house, piping hot scones straight out of the oven with jam and cream were waiting. Everyone was impressed and it was quick and easy. Of course you don't have the same amount of lead time as I do — it doesn't take twelve minutes for a visitor to pull into your front drive, like it does for a plane to circle and land at Bullo — but don't dismiss scones. They are always a favourite and some old favourites just keep going forever.

Bullo River Scones

The following is a good basic scone recipe.

2 cups/250 g self-raising flour
pinch of salt
60 g butter, cut into small pieces
1 tablespoon white sugar
milk to mix, could be up to 1 cup

Sift flour and salt into a mixing bowl. Add butter and rub into the flour between the fingertips and thumbs. Add the sugar.

Add the milk gradually and mix to a soft consistency, using a round-bladed knife.

Tip dough onto a floured surface and pat into a round shape, 2.5 cm thick. Cut the scones out with a scone cutter and put on an ungreased, lightly floured baking tray.

Bake in a very hot oven/220°C, for around 8 to 12 minutes, until cooked. The scones are cooked when they are firm to the touch. Cool on a wire cooling rack and serve while freshly made.

MAKES 12 – 16 APPROXIMATELY

To make good scones you have to remember:
- A good scone dough should not be too stiff, it should leave the fingers sticky when mixing and be quite soft to touch.
- Do not roll scones too much. Pat quickly into shape, cut to size, bake straight away.
- Use a very hot oven.

Variations:
- You can add ¼ – ½ cup sultanas.
- You can add ¼ – ½ cup currants.
- You can make a hole in the centre of each scone and add a dob of jam.
- You can leave out the sugar and use the same quantity of golden syrup. You will need less milk, but don't cut down on the milk too much; keep the mixture sticky to give you a nice moist scone. Grease the baking tray.

The stockcamp manages to go through trays and trays of all kinds of scones per day. But we still need to cook the regular meals that 'stick to the ribs'. A 'stick to the ribs' meal is one with a good deal of sustenance, food that will keep the men going during the hard working day. Oxtail Stew is such a recipe.

I always smile when I read the line 'cut oxtail through at each joint'. Many years ago, when I was full-time cook, I was chopping the oxtail in the kitchen when a young boy we had working on the station walked in with a message from Uncle Dick.

He stopped short in the middle of relaying the message, a look of complete amazement on his face, and exclaimed, 'Gee, that's some knife! It's cutting straight through the bone, just like it was butter! Gee, I ain't never seen nothun like that!'

I looked up and saw that he was serious – he didn't know the tail had joints all along it. He really did think I was cutting through solid bone!

Oxtail Stew

A Bullo regular.

1 oxtail
½ cup plain flour
pinch of dried mixed herbs
pinch of ground cloves
½ teaspoon salt
¼ teaspoon black pepper
3 tablespoons olive oil
2 tablespoons butter
3 cups hot water
2 cups red wine
12 black peppercorns
2 bay leaves
2 cloves
⅓ cup pearl barley
2 stalks celery, sliced
2 onions, thinly sliced
2 carrots, sliced
1 teaspoon Worcestershire sauce

Cut oxtail through at each joint or have the butcher cut it for you. Trim each piece, cut off all surplus fat and rinse well.

In a bowl, mix flour with mixed herbs, ground cloves, salt and pepper. Coat the oxtail with seasoned flour.

In a large, heavy-based frying pan, heat oil and butter. Add the oxtail pieces and brown on all sides. Remove from pan and drain on paper towels.

Put the oxtail in a large, heavy-based pan; add the hot water, wine, peppercorns, bay leaves and cloves. Cover, bring to the boil, reduce heat and simmer for 3 hours.

Let cool, then chill until the fat hardens on top. Lift fat from the surface and discard; transfer oxtail pieces to a plate. Strain the liquid through a fine strainer to catch the cloves, peppercorns and bay leaves. Return liquid to pan; add barley, celery, onions, carrots, oxtail and Worcestershire sauce.

Simmer, covered, for a further 1 hour, until vegetables are tender. The oxtail should be tender by now, and easy to pull off the bone. The consistency is between a thick soup and a stew. Depending on your preference, thicken accordingly. You can do this with cornflour blended smoothly with a little cold water. Stir into the stew and simmer for a further 4 minutes.

Serve with crunchy hot bread, as a soup, or with rice or potatoes as a stew.

SERVES 6

Sometimes the most unlikely people surprise you. One such girl was a distant relative from America. Her mother wrote me such a nice letter, explaining how we were related (she was Charlie's cousin, twice removed) and wondered if her daughter could visit the station for three months, in between finishing college and starting university.

Holly arrived, very sweet and intelligent, but completely useless in an outback environment. Lucky for us she wanted to learn, and so we started to teach her.

Her first job was to learn to milk Daisy, our milking cow. This she did very slowly, but in time she wasn't too bad. Of course Daisy demanded extra food for standing still for so long as Holly laboured hard to increase her milking speed. After about half an hour Daily got a bit short tempered, even with the extra food supply, so Holly tried singing to her. Daisy loved it and would stand for hours listening to Holly sing.

One day Holly came into the kitchen, worried and exclaiming that Daisy didn't have any milk. I had seen Daisy walk past the kitchen a few minutes before — she definitely had milk.

I went outside, milked Daisy and out came the milk.

'But I tried, and nothing came out,' said a frustrated Holly.

'Daisy is very temperamental. Are you doing anything different, like changing her feed bucket or putting in different food?' I asked.

'No,' replied Holly to each of my questions.

'Well, I can't stay. Try and work it out — she definitely has milk, you just have to be stern with her sometimes. Let me finish what I am doing and if she is still misbehaving, I will have to milk her, she won't hold the milk back with me.' Daisy was very smart, she knew who she could con and who she had to behave for.

Holly came into the kitchen all smiles — she had solved the mystery. Daisy was holding back the milk because Holly wasn't singing. When Holly's lovely voice rang out across the paddock, Daisy's milk flowed.

Holly's move to the kitchen was by chance. One day when I was particularly busy, she offered to help.

'What can you do?' I asked hopefully.

'Nothing, really. But I would like to learn.' And she did.

The next night I told the men, 'Sorry, no dessert tonight. It was one of "those" days, but there are scones and cake in the fridge.'

The next morning Holly said maybe she could make the dessert each day for me. 'Great', was my reply, 'go for your life.'

The stockmen were amazingly patient and ate some colossal failures, after Holly produced something that was far removed from what the recipe said she should have produced.

'What have I done?' became a regular remark in the kitchen for the next few weeks. But she persevered and won through.

The men went from saying, 'Oh, I might skip dessert tonight' to, 'What's on tonight, Hol?' Her desserts were something they now looked forward to as everyone followed her progress. It was a great help to me as not cooking a dessert each night gave me some extra time, so I was thrilled with her progress.

She also grew in confidence, something I discovered one day when she said, 'I'd like to try this.' Holly was holding a cookbook open at the recipe for Danish Pastry! I told her that even I wouldn't try that, but this did not deter her. After many failures I suggested that maybe she should wait until the weather was cooler because it really was not the month to be making pastry as her hands were too hot.

However, Holly was determined to perfect Danish Pastry before she went back to America. She attacked the recipe again but this time with a bowl of ice cubes at her side. Every time before she touched the pastry she froze her hands in the ice first. Holly's hands looked like prunes, mind you, but the stockcamp ate light, fluffy Danish Pastries, as good as anything out of the best bakery, and they were delighted.

Holly went home and wowed her family with her culinary expertise. She offered to cook the cakes for a big family party. The entire family just couldn't believe what a great cook she was and the Danish Pastries were the hit of the party.

Holly still sends an annual Christmas card and a catch-up letter now and then, telling us what she is doing with her life. She wanted to be a singer, so after university she went to New York to make it big. She worked at a

Opposite: Oxtail Stew (recipe page 102). Following pages: Sunrise at Six Mile Crossing (where saltwater meets freshwater), Bullo River. Fresh Barra, Straight out of the River (recipe page 208) with Mushroom and Olive Salad (recipe page 38).

normal job during the day and took whatever she could at night in the way of singing engagements. As she found out, it was not easy. Her letters told of how she gave herself a lift when things were glum by making Bullo River Bread, scones or Danish Pastries.

A delightful letter described how one gloomy, rainy Sunday afternoon she was sitting in her lonely apartment, feeling down, so she decided to bake some bread.

Holly was new in the building, knew no-one and was surprised that no-one spoke in the elevators. People just hurried into their apartments, closed the door and kept to themselves. But a miraculous thing happened when she baked her Bullo River Bread. The wonderful smell of freshly baking bread wafted through the building and soon people were knocking at her door with a pretext like 'she was new in the building – did she know where the garbage disposal was?' or 'did she know how to find the fire escape?' Then, ever so casually, they'd say, 'Oh, I can smell fresh bread; are you baking bread?'

Holly went from a lonely afternoon to having half the building in her apartment eating bread, drinking wine and just talking to each other!

People started talking in the elevators and weekends became social events. Holly told of her life at Bullo River, showed photos in the little apartment in New York of the vast plains of the outback of Australia. The building constantly had a wonderful bread baking aroma drifting through it and people talked ... all because of a loaf of bread cooking.

Cooked by a girl from Boston, who learned to cook bread on an outback cattle station, in Australia, who was a bit down on a lonely, rainy afternoon in New York City.

Food is a powerful mediator.

It was Sunday and my turn to cook, but being Mother's Day Marlee surprised me with a marvellous lunch. I am allowed to have all the 'naughty' things on my birthday and Mother's Day so I really enjoy myself. Although being naughty is nice, I'm slowly teaching myself to indulge to a degree, and still thoroughly enjoy the meal, but to not go right off the scale, in terms of fat consumption and calories.

Opposite: My Mum's Lemon Dumplings (recipe page 107).

I love garlic prawns, so that was the first course. The words 'Garlic Prawns' conjures up the image of prawns bubbling in a sea of butter. I decided cook it without the sea of butter and the three thousand calories.

Garlic Prawns

3 teaspoons olive oil

6 garlic cloves, crushed

4 spring onions/shallots, thinly sliced

1 kg fresh green prawns, shelled and deveined

1 cup chopped fresh parsley

2 tablespoons butter

Heat a heavy-based frying pan until hot, add 1 teaspoon olive oil. Reduce heat to medium-low, add garlic and cook until golden brown, stirring frequently. Do not burn.

Remove garlic from pan and set aside. Add the spring onions to the pan and cook lightly; set aside.

Return the heat to high and add the remaining oil and some prawns, just enough to cover the pan in a single layer. Cook prawns on one side, and, when you see the colour of the prawn has changed halfway up the prawn, turn it over. When prawns are cooked, remove quickly. Keep warm while cooking the rest in the same way.

When all the prawns are cooked, return them to the hot pan, off the heat; add the spring onions, garlic and parsley; toss to mix. Put butter, in small dobs, over the prawns; let it melt. Toss prawns again and serve immediately. Rice and green salad go perfectly with my style of garlic prawns!

SERVES 4

My Mum always made this, my favourite dessert, whenever I came home for a visit. I grew up loving this dessert and still do to this day. Marlee made it for my Mother's Day lunch, followed by most amazingly delicious cake.

My Mum's Lemon Dumplings

Dumplings:

1¼ cups self-raising flour

30 g butter

2 teaspoons grated lemon rind

⅓ cup golden syrup

⅓ cup milk

10 blanched almonds

¼ tart apple, peeled and cored

Lemon Sauce:

30 g unsalted butter

½ cup light brown sugar

½ cup golden syrup

1 cup water

1 cup mixed fresh lemon and fresh lime juice including 3 tablespoons orange juice

2 tablespoons each grated lemon and orange rind

To make Dumplings: Sift flour into a mixing bowl, add butter and rub in with the fingertips and thumbs. Make a well (hollow) in the middle of the flour. Mix almonds and apple together in a food processor to form a puree.

Combine lemon rind, golden syrup, milk and almond–apple puree in a small bowl. Mix well. Stir this mixture into the flour until you have a moist dough.

Using lightly floured fingers, shape rounded table-spoons of mixture into balls.

To make Lemon Sauce: Combine butter, sugar, golden syrup, water, mixed citrus juice and rind in a saucepan. Stir over a medium heat until butter is melted; bring to the boil. Reduce heat to low and simmer for 5 minutes.

Pour the sauce into a warm, greased, shallow casserole dish with a lid. Add the dumplings, in a single layer.

Cover and cook in a moderate oven/180°C, for about 30 minutes.

Serve the dumplings warm, with sauce spooned over them. Accompany with cream or ice cream if liked.

SERVES 6

Bullo Dream Layered Cake

170 g plain flour

¼ teaspoon baking powder
minus a pinch

225 g unsalted butter, softened
to room temperature

¾ cup caster sugar

3 large eggs, separated

85 g dark cooking chocolate,
melted in a double-boiler

Filling:

25 g unsalted butter

75 g fresh fine wholemeal
breadcrumbs

300 ml fresh or thickened
cream

1 teaspoon vanilla sugar

100 g dark cooking chocolate

5 tablespoons strawberry jam

2 cups purée of mixed
blueberries, raspberries and
strawberries

extra fresh berries for
decoration

Sift together the flour and baking powder and set aside.

Beat butter with an electric mixer until it is creamy. Add the sugar and continue beating until the mixture is light and fluffy. Add egg yolks and beat until they are mixed in well. Add the dry ingredients and stir gently until evenly mixed and smooth.

Whisk the egg whites until they hold firm peaks. Carefully stir the chocolate into the cake mixture. Fold about a third of the whisked egg whites into the mixture, then fold in the remaining egg whites.

Spoon the mixture into a lined and greased 21 x 11 x 6 cm loaf tin. Bake in a moderately slow oven/160°C for about 1 hour and 20 minutes. Rotate the tin about halfway through the cooking time.

Allow the cake to cool for 10 minutes in the tin before turning out onto a wire cooling rack to cool completely. When cool, slice into 3 horizontal layers.

To make Filling: Melt butter in a heavy-based frying pan over a medium heat. Add the breadcrumbs and cook until crisp and browned, stirring frequently. Remove from pan and set aside until cool.

Whip cream with vanilla sugar until thick. Grate the chocolate. Carefully fold together the breadcrumbs, whipped cream and three-quarters of the chocolate.

On the bottom layer, spread half the strawberry jam, some berry purée, then a third of the cream mixture. Cover with another layer of cake and repeat. Put the top layer on and spread with remaining cream mixture; sprinkle with remaining grated chocolate and decorate with fresh berries. Serve with remaining berry purée.

SERVES 8 – 12

Cool mornings find us looking for a cover at 3.00 am – we know winter is finally here. When the first cold snap hits in the morning we are never ready for it. After sleeping without covers for so many months, we're sure winter will never come.

We wake sometimes wrapped in some strange things that we have sleepily grabbed in the early hours to keep us warm.

The skies are now clear of clouds every morning, baby blue for as far as the eye can see, with not a blemish anywhere. Mist and fog swirl into the valley just before sunrise as moving warm and cold air collide in the valley bed. You can be sitting for a quiet moment sipping that first cup of coffee, admiring the hills and distant horizon when suddenly, the entire scene disappears before your eyes. It happens that fast.

The early morning with fog spreading over the valley is a lovely time, so quiet and peaceful. As open as the house is, the fog stays outside; only a few times, when it was as 'thick as pea soup' did it come into the house and we had trouble finding the phone when it was ringing.

As I sip my coffee, watching the fog lift, it brings back memories of Charlie. Wherever he was, he caused chaos, even making a simple cup of coffee. During the last ten years of his life his eyes were quite bad, so if he didn't wear glasses when making a cup of coffee, it caused major problems.

Charlie's theory was, 'if it's in a jug, it has to be milk'. There was no walk-in chiller in those days; everything had to be stored in the fridges. To save space we put lots of things, other than milk, in jugs but no-one could convince Charlie to look in the jug before pouring.

Over the years he made me coffee with custard, chicken gravy, pancake mix, apple puree, yoghurt, yeast mixture and vanilla milkshake instead of milk. If it was in a jug, it had to be milk. What's more, he supported this theory by drinking every terrible concoction he made. I think he had trouble with more than his eyes!

By the end of May the mornings were getting decidedly cold, winter was settling in, and we still didn't have a cook.

June

Steak – Kidney – Liver, Bullo-Style

~

Marinated Steak

~

Orange Glazed Carrots

~

Parsnip and Turnip Cakes

~

Crusty Sweet Potato Casserole

~

Fresh Tomato Soup with Dill

~

Leg of Lamb with Herb Crust

~

Almond-Crumbed Fish

~

Green Ginger Sauce

~

Citrus Coffee and Hazelnut Pudding

~

Coffee Liqueur Cream Sauce

~

'Well, I don't know what we are going to do. I have to leave for Sydney tomorrow.'

'I have at least another week's work before the road is opened and we have that shipment of steers due to go out next week. I must keep going, the road has to be open for the trains.'

'Just once I would like to get someone who can cook! All the girls who apply for the job just can't cook!'

Marlee and I sat there looking glumly into our coffee, trying to work out how we could get meals on the table in the following week and still do all the things that needed to be done.

'I'll do it,' said a quiet voice. It was Gail, one of the girls helping Marlee with the horses.

'You can cook?' we asked together.

'Yes,' came the short reply. Working on the theory we used when hiring stockmen (the less they said, the more they could do), we accepted the offer.

'Why did you watch all these hopeless cooks come and go and not say anything?'

'Don't like cooking.' Gail was a girl of few words. 'I want to work outside with the animals.'

Marlee and I had no arguments with that statement: these were our sentiments exactly.

I left for Sydney the next morning and spoke to Marlee that night.

'How's the new cook?'

Marlee went on and on. 'Great food, Gail is so organised she even has time to work outside!'

'Will she cook all season?' I asked quickly.

'No, just until we find someone.'

So the next cook arrived, and we were plunged from the bliss of good meals, a clean kitchen and freedom for Marlee and me into living hell.

She wanted to know what days she could have to go shopping. When we said the food came in by plane and that she didn't go shopping, she was most upset — she always did her own shopping! The 1200 kilometres to the nearest supermarket was explained, but it turned out she needed to go to town for more than shopping.

During her short stay she cut up two whole fillet steaks and fed them to the dogs. When asked why she'd used the fillet steak for dog meat, her reply was that it looked scraggy and she thought it was meat scraps. The fact that there was a blue plastic tag hanging on the hook with the meat saying 'fillet steak' didn't seem to have much significance. She had to be monitored constantly, after it was discovered she had wiped out the entire supply of cooking sherry in one morning — not on cooking.

Her attitude left a lot to be desired; you could feel her thinking, 'you've got meat everywhere, what's your problem?' It didn't worry her in the least that there wasn't a decent dinner ready for the crew when they came in tired and hungry at the end of the day.

One day Marlee had left a stew for the dogs simmering on the stove, made out of the leftovers that were piling up in the fridge at an alarming rate. The girl had no idea of quantities, so Marlee removed a lot of the food and made it into a dog stew (otherwise she could see us living on warmed up leftovers for evermore). The cook served it to the men for lunch with rice and vegetables. Luckily, the food was good. We arrived back late to find the dog's stew gone.

The final straw came when Franz brought in the meat from a new 'killer' (a steer killed for meat to eat). He boned out the animal and laid out the cuts on the kitchen bench. The cook's job was to label everything, hang the good cuts in the chiller, freeze the tougher cuts, make some into mince meat, package the dogs' meat and then pack it all neatly away in the freezer.

'What's that?' she asked curtly.

'What's it look like?' Franz was equally short.

'I know what it is,' she sneered, 'but what is it doing there?'

Franz patiently explained that it was there for her to put away.

'I don't touch hot meat,' came the reply.

Franz told her it was the cook's job to put the meat away and that if she wanted to stay the cook, she had better put the meat away.

She refused and departed – no-one was sad to see her leave. Wonderful Gail stepped in again for a few weeks, until the next cook, and everyone was deliriously happy.

But there were times when Gail helped in the stockyards with the rest of the crew, so I would fill the breach, cooking a quick, solid meal for a crew of hungry people back from working all day with cattle in hot, dusty yards.

The following recipe is one such meal. There is nothing as good as a plain grill! And most meats and fish can be just plain pan-grilled. A good heavy-based frying pan or griddle pan is essential.

Steak – Kidney – Liver, Bullo-Style

Steak

Grease the pan with a piece of fat from the beef steak. Heat pan; add 1 crushed garlic clove and cook for a few minutes. Remove all the garlic.

Heat the pan until very, very hot. Select beef steaks which are about 2.5 cm thick. Do not trim all the fat from the steak. Put the steak in the pan. Let it cook undisturbed until you see the colour change on the bottom and halfway up the side of the steak, then sprinkle top of each steak lightly with mustard powder and ¼ teaspoon Worcestershire sauce.

Turn steak over; continue cooking for a few minutes, until there is a total colour change. This results in a medium-rare steak, so if you like your steak well-done, leave it a little longer on a lower heat until cooked to taste.

Do not turn steak more than once.

Now trim all fat off steak, sprinkle the second side lightly with mustard, Worcestershire sauce and chopped fresh parsley and serve straight from the pan to the plate.

Kidneys

Follow the hot pan and cooked garlic method as above, then pan-grill thin 8 cm slices in the very hot pan for a few minutes, turning once, until colour changes and kidney is cooked through. Serve immediately.

Liver

Follow the hot pan and garlic method as above. Slice liver thinner than kidney, about 5 mm thick. Sprinkle one side of slices with basil. Cook in the very hot pan on one side, for 1 minute, then turn over and cook on the other side for a further 1 minute. Sprinkle lightly with fresh chopped basil and serve straight from the pan to the plate.

I have read that liver is very good for you; after breadfruit it is the most complete food you can eat, loaded with all the minerals and trace elements your body needs. The article went on to say you should eat it once a week. Beef liver has a much stronger and nicer flavour than the smaller livers. Most people usually say, 'Yuck! Liver, no thanks.' If you are one of these people, give our Bullo-Style Liver a try. We had one stockman who informed me that he violently disliked liver and never ate the stuff.

I served liver cooked as above and he ate it for months before someone told him it was liver. He kept remarking, 'This is the tenderest steak I have ever eaten.' Of course when he found out it was liver he wouldn't touch it again, despite the fact he ate and enjoyed it for months.

A plain grill is great, but often we feel like something a little more tasty. If you like your steak marinated, the following recipe is for you.

Marinated Steak

Marinade:

2 large cloves garlic, crushed

5 teaspoons sake or dry sherry

1 teaspoon grated ginger

1 cup light or reduced-salt soy sauce

1 cup chicken stock

3 teaspoons honey

2 teaspoons cornflour blended smoothly with 3 teaspoons cold water

Steak:

750 g rump or fillet beef steak, thinly sliced

2 tablespoons peanut oil

To make Marinade: place all ingredients in a mixing bowl; mix well. Add sliced steak to marinade; stir to coat well. Cover and marinate in the refrigerator for 30 minutes, at least.

Heat oil in a wok or a heavy-based frying pan or griddle pan. When wok or pan is very, very hot, add only a few slices of steak at a time and cook quickly until colour changes. Serve straight from pan to the plate.

Serves 4 – 6

Note: This marinade can be used for almost any meat, fish or chicken, but it is *not suitable* for kidneys or liver.

It has surprised me over the years how many people don't like vegetables, especially men. I will serve a meal of meat, potatoes, carrots, pumpkin, greens, salad and bread: the meat, potatoes and bread disappear, but the rest of the serving dishes remain untouched.

So I set about to try and make vegetables acceptable to the stockmen. The following recipes are what I came up with.

Orange Glazed Carrots

*500 g fresh carrots, sliced
or cut in 'sticks'*

1 chicken stock cube

1 teaspoon brown sugar

1 teaspoon butter

*chopped fresh parsley for
garnish*

Sauce

60 g butter

1 tablespoon cornflour

2 tablespoons honey

2 tablespoons vinegar

*grated rind and juice of
1 orange*

Place carrots in a pan with just 2 cm boiling water. Crumble stock cube over the carrots. Add sugar and butter and cook, covered, until tender. Watch to see water doesn't run dry. If lid is tight-fitting the carrots should steam and the liquid will not evaporate, but just watch and add a little more water if necessary.

To make the Sauce: Soften butter and honey in a saucepan over a medium heat. Mix cornflour in a small bowl with a little vinegar to make a paste, then add the rest of the vinegar, orange rind and juice. Add to saucepan and stir over a medium heat for 5 minutes, or until sauce boils and thickens.

Drain carrots and add to the sauce. Toss carrots lightly and serve sprinkled with chopped parsley.

SERVES 4

Parsnip and Turnip Cakes

1 cup cooked parsnips

1 cup cooked turnips

1 egg, beaten

1 tablespoon milk

¼ plain flour

salt and black pepper to taste

¼ teaspoon ground nutmeg

Combine all ingredients in a mixing bowl and beat until light and fluffy. Level mixture and divide into equal portions. Shape each portion into a flat cake.

Pan-grill cakes in a very hot, oiled frying pan or griddle pan. Cook until golden brown on each side and heated through. Serve immediately.

SERVES 4 – 6

There is no-one more distrusting than a stockman if he thinks you are trying to put something over him, especially when it comes to food. A stockman likes what he likes and that about covers it. To try and change their likes and dislikes is near impossible.

'What's this?' they asked when I served the Orange Glazed Carrots and the Parsnip and Turnip Cakes.

'Food. Try it.'

Eventually they did and liked it. 'Geez, I ain't never tasted vegies like this.'

The following sweet potato recipe is a top favourite. The plain sweet potatoes were always left untouched. This one goes in a flash.

Crusty Sweet Potato Casserole

3 cups cooked and mashed sweet potatoes

½ teaspoon salt

40 g butter

1 teaspoon vanilla essence

½ cup milk

2 eggs, lightly beaten

½ cup light brown sugar

½ cup self-raising flour

extra 40 g butter, chilled and diced

1 cup chopped mixed nuts, almonds, walnuts and hazelnuts

Combine sweet potatoes, salt, butter, vanilla, milk and eggs in a mixing bowl and beat together, with a wooden spoon, until smooth. Pour into a casserole dish.

In a small bowl, mix together brown sugar, flour, and nuts. Rub extra butter into flour mixture. Sprinkle mixture over the potato mixture.

Bake in a slow oven/150°F for 30–35 minutes or until brown and crunchy on the top.

SERVES 6

Opposite: Orange Glazed Carrots (recipe page 119), Parsnip and Turnip Cakes (recipe page 119) and Crusty Sweet Potato Casserole (recipe this page). Following pages: Bullo-Style Steak (recipe page 116).

By June the weather is freezing cold and we huddle under blankets and doonas. It is 8° every morning. For breakfast, we can't get enough hot food: porridge, beans on toast, savoury mince, eggs and bacon.

Everyone walks around in jumpers, thick jackets and padded vests, complaining of freezing cold hands. Skies are cloudless and heavy fog envelops the valley each morning. The grass is a sea of silver, the dew so wet and heavy it bows the blades of grass to the ground.

Riding boots walking across the lawn leave green footprints on a silver sea.

The sun, so meek and mild in comparison to its summer face, takes until 10.00 am to make its presence felt. By then the temperature reaches a cool 18°C, the dew has vanished and the paddocks are a sea of normal green again.

Soups feature on the menu. There are a few tins of soup in the pantry for emergencies and for 'going bush', but most of our soups are homemade.

Fresh Tomato Soup with Dill

2 tablespoons olive oil

2 onions, thinly sliced

1½ teaspoons fresh dill

6 cups chopped tomatoes

⅓ cup tomato paste

1 cup beef stock

1 cup chicken stock

1 tablespoon brown sugar

2 tablespoons chopped fresh parsley

grated rind and juice of ½ lemon

freshly ground black pepper to taste

chopped fresh parsley and fresh dill sprigs for garnish

Heat oil in a large, heavy-based pan, add onion and cook over a medium heat until soft and transparent. Add dill, tomatoes and tomato paste. Cover and simmer over a medium-low heat for 30 minutes.

Cool mixture slightly, then put into a blender or food processor and mix until fairly smooth.

Pour pureé into pan and add beef and chicken stocks, sugar, parsley, lemon rind and juice, and pepper to taste. Bring to the boil and simmer for 5 minutes.

Serve soup hot garnished with chopped parsley and sprigs of dill. Accompany with garlic croutons if liked, (see recipe on page 25).

SERVES 4 – 6

Opposite: Fresh Tomato Soup with Dill (recipe this page).

Hot spicy foods are back on the menu and are something that we look forward to at night. As soon as the sun sets the temperature goes into a spiral dive. It can drop 15° in a few minutes. We will be sitting in shorts and a cotton shirt at a pleasant temperature of 24°C, then like an invisible wave, cold air invades the room, and in the blink of an eye we are shivering in a chilly 10°. No cold roast beef and salads on these nights; it's hot food and if it's hot and spicy, all the better. Even Franz is not looking for the compulsory salad on a June night.

Baked dinners can be served for lunch now that the weather is so cool and the men welcome a hot, 'stick to your ribs' meal to keep them going for the rest of the day.

There is never a truer saying than 'variety is the spice of life'. When the people first arrive to start the season and sit down to a hefty steak for dinner, the comments are, 'Oh beauty, steak!' and for a roast beef dinner, 'Wow, roast beef!'

Just a few weeks later it turns to, 'Struth! Not steak again,' and 'Can't we have something else beside beef?'

We learned this lesson many years ago and now we try to weave an occasional meal of chicken or lamb through the menu.

When we serve the following baked lamb, the aroma reaches into the far corners of the nearby paddocks and no-one is late for dinner. There is a stampede to be first at the carving plate.

Leg of Lamb with Herb Crust

2 teaspoons ground cumin

2 teaspoons ground coriander

¼ teaspoon ground cinnamon

¼ teaspoon salt

freshly ground pepper

1.5 kg leg of lamb

2 cloves garlic, crushed

2 tablespoons chopped fresh
parsley

2 tablespoons chopped fresh
rosemary

2 teaspoons chopped fresh
chives

2 teaspoons brown sugar

1 teaspoon mustard powder

1 teaspoon Worcestershire sauce

½ cup day-old breadcrumbs

1 chicken stock cube, crumbled

juice of ½ lemon

30 g butter, melted

Mix together the cumin, coriander, cinnamon, salt and pepper to taste in a small bowl. Rub spice mixture over the lamb with clean fingers.

In a greased roasting pan, brown the lamb on all sides, over a medium heat on the stovetop, until nicely browned.

Combine the garlic, parsley, rosemary, chives, sugar, mustard, Worcestershire sauce, breadcrumbs, stock cube, lemon juice and melted butter in a bowl. Mix well. If not moist enough add more butter and lemon juice.

Make a few slits on top of the leg of lamb and press in some of the herb mixture. Coat the top of the leg with the remaining mixture, pressing on well to stick.

Place lamb on a rack in the roasting pan and roast in a moderate oven/180°C for about 1½ hours, or until cooked through. Place on a serving platter and keep warm.

Make a gravy with the pan juices mixed with flour, stock and seasonings.

Carve the lamb at the table and serve with gravy, mint sauce, roast potatoes, sweet potatoes and a green vegetable.

SERVES 6 – 8

Because there is also an endless supply of barra, we get the same remarks as we do about the beef.

'Strike me blimey, not barra again!'

So the search for variety goes on. Here is another way we serve barra, but it can be used for other fish as well.

Almond-Crumbed Fish

6 white fish fillets, skinned
2 tablespoons lemon juice
30 g butter
125 g slivered almonds
2 cups fresh breadcrumbs
¼ cup chopped fresh parsley
salt and white pepper
1 egg, lightly beaten
¼ cup milk
½ cup plain flour
3 tablespoons olive oil
lemon wedges for serving

Place fish in a shallow dish, pour lemon juice over and let stand for 10 minutes.

Heat a heavy-based frying pan over a low heat and add 1 teaspoon butter and the almonds; stir constantly until almonds are golden. Do not burn. Remove from pan and drain on paper towels. Cool, then chop finely.

Combine breadcrumbs, almonds, parsley, salt and pepper to taste in a shallow bowl. Mix well. Combine beaten egg with milk; mix well. Pour egg mixture into a shallow bowl. Place flour on a sheet of grease-proof paper.

Remove fish from lemon juice and coat with flour. Dip the floured fish in the egg mixture, then coat with the almond-crumb mixture. Press the mixture onto fish by lightly rolling each side with a rolling pin.

Heat oil and remaining butter in the frying pan, add fish fillets and cook gently over a medium–low heat, turning once, until golden brown on both sides and cooked through.

Serve fish with lemon wedges, Green Ginger Sauce, rice and salad or green vegetables.

SERVES 6

Green Ginger Sauce

1 cup mayonnaise

2 teaspoons lemon juice

2 teaspoons grated ginger

¼ cup chopped fresh parsley

white pepper to taste

⅓ cup sour cream

Combine all ingredients in a bowl and mix well. Cover and refrigerate the sauce until ready to serve.

Serve with Almond-Crumbed Fish.

I cannot put anything in our oven without thinking of Uncle Dick. Our dear old electric oven is something to see. It is around twenty years old and was one of the first 'self-clean' ovens to hit the market – only ours never worked.

The first time I decided to clean it I followed the instructions, waited and then looked inside, expecting to see what a clean oven I had without even lifting a finger. Instead, I received quite a shock. The shiny enamel surface had just disintegrated, peeled off and fluttered down into a heap at the bottom of the oven.

The cleaning procedure had worked so well it had removed the lining of the oven as well as the grease! The makers would not replace the oven until I sent it south. I wanted a replacement first and then they could have it. The arguments went back and forth until I just had no choice but to live with a rust-lined oven.

A few months later the glass door exploded all over the kitchen. The makers received a terse communication and they quickly dispatched a new oven door.

Uncle Dick installed the new door and left his personal stamp – you could say it was an 'Uncle Dick curiosity'. The oven door never closed properly again, so a wedge had to be made. This was lost over the years, so most of the time you had to stuff in a tea towel to stop the door from falling open. He also repaired the griller and from then onwards, it only ever half worked. No matter how many elements were replaced, you could only cook in the front part of the grill.

The next problem was the thermostat, which also stopped working. Dick fitted the new one, it worked okay, but there was a hitch. You needed a pad and pencil to work out the mathematics required to set the dial at the right temperature. The dial registered the right numbers but the power didn't switch on until the needle passed 203° Fahrenheit.

Over the years the complicated procedures became second nature to us, but trying to explain all of Uncle Dick's 'adjustments' to a new cook – who wasn't too sure how to cook rice – was near impossible.

So whenever the oven or grill were needed, Marlee or I would have to be at the controls. As inconvenient as it was to have to race to the kitchen every time these appliances were needed, it was better than eating a half-cooked roast or a flat, leathery cake.

Despite all this the poor old oven is still in there cooking up a storm; well, sometimes we have to give it an extra fifteen minutes on the recipe time. In a strange way I will miss the old oven; we have been through so much together.

Another kitchen appliance that visited Uncle Dick's workshop and was never the same again was the mixer. It was a heavy-duty model, but it still couldn't keep up with the demands the Bullo kitchen made on it.

It worked faithfully along with the oven for many years, mixing the cakes that the oven cooked. Both appliances should be in the *Guinness Book of Records*.

Halfway through its life it needed a new drive belt but it returned from the workshop a 'changed' mixer. It still worked quite well, but somewhere along the line a metamorphosis had occurred and the mixer now thought it was a jet. When it started up the noise was deafening; speech was impossible two rooms away. We put up with this for so long we didn't realise there were normal mixers out there that didn't sound like jets.

Stockmen in the paddocks for kilometres around knew when the kitchen was mixing a cake. The noise was amazing and we put up with it for ten years. It was finally laid to rest last year.

The funniest of all of Uncle Dick's repairs had to be the toaster. After he replaced the spring toast would soar across the kitchen when cooked. However, like all things on the station, the kitchen has moved ahead. We now receive compliments on what a nice kitchen we have. We have come a long way from the days of the tin shed with the fire-breathing monster in the corner.

That old wood stove is still around, believe it or not. It is down in the staff quarters (soon to be demolished) having been used over the years as an open fireplace.

What memories that old stove brings back! It baked the best bread possible, was the best place to roast a whole rump and the only way to cook a cake. In fact no stove cooks better than a wood stove; it produces a flavour that cannot be duplicated by any modern engineering.

The only drawback to using a wooden stove in the tropics is the heat. Cooking in front of a wood-burning stove is so hot, I can't find the words to describe the torture, especially when the stove is in the corner of a tin shed.

Uncle Dick couldn't watch me suffer any longer, so he decided to take action. He moved the stove outside and built a sandstone bench completely around it so I didn't lose pots over the side any more. It ended up as an outside barbecue, next to the kitchen.

It was wonderful in the winter months, but the problems started when summer arrived. I was standing in the sun all day and it was as hot as being in the tin shed. I also had the added risk of developing skin cancer at a fast rate! Dick rigged a canvas awning over the stove and although the heat was still there, at least I was in the shade.

But the fun really started when the rainy season arrived. The storms would hit at five o'clock on the dot and I'd be standing in the rain, soaked to the skin, cooking dinner and holding an umbrella over the stove to stop the fire going out.

One evening when I was battling with the wind and umbrella I was almost at the end of my tether. It had been 'one of those days' and the men were sitting out of the rain, relaxed and comfortable and drinking a beer while waiting for their dinner. Charlie looked across at me, laughed and remarked, 'Well, you said that you wanted to be cool when you cooked – it looks like you got that wish.' It was the last straw.

I stopped my battle with the wind, looked at Charlie and was about to tell him what he could do with the cooking job, when the rope on the canvas awning broke and dumped litres of accumulated rain water over me.

Charlie laughed until he fell off his chair, asking me in between gasps and fits of laughter was I 'cool enough'?

I was too tired to get angry. I looked down at the stove. The steak was floating around in a frying pan full of water and the rest of the pots were overflowing. Peas, carrots and potatoes were spilling onto the stove and then cascading over the edge into the dirt on the ground. The stove was hissing and steaming, the fire was out and I had had enough.

I quietly folded the umbrella, hung the plastic apron on a nail and walked to my bedroom.

I could hear Charlie's voice chiding me for being a bad sport and then, when he realised the consequences of having no cook, pleading forgiveness. I just kept walking.

Charlie appeared at the bedroom door.

'What about dinner?'

'What about it? It's there, serve yourself.'

'But it's a mess!'

'Bad luck. Get another cook and see if she'll cook under those conditions. You might not realise it, but I just quit.'

I heard him casually telling the men he thought I was coming down with something and to serve themselves. Grumblings drifted from the kitchen as the men tried to salvage something to eat from the waterlogged meal.

The next day we went to town to pick out my new oven and cooktop. As much as I loved the way the old wood stove cooked, the bliss of the new oven and cooktop was heavenly. I still used the wood stove in the winter, when it felt good to be warmed by the heat it radiated.

Everyone enjoys the cold weather. One of the most exciting things about the weather change is that we can make the cake recipes we couldn't even think of making during the hot months.

Butter can now sit on the table for an hour or so without turning into a puddle of grease; cream stays whipped and on the cake. So we start thinking about those marvellous desserts and cakes that are covered with coatings of 'energy-giving substance' – in other words, cream.

Hot desserts are one of the favourites and puddings are top of the list. A very extra-special favourite follows.

Citrus Coffee and Hazelnut Pudding

½ cup self-raising flour

½ cup day-old cake crumbs

½ cup ground hazelnuts

4 large eggs, separated

½ cup light brown sugar

1 teaspoon vanilla
flavouring essence

1 tablespoon grated lemon
rind

1 tablespoon grated orange
rind

1 tablespoon instant coffee
granules

1 tablespoon hot water

extra ground hazelnuts for
sprinkling

Grease 6 x 250 ml pudding moulds or souffle dishes.

Sift flour into a mixing bowl and stir in cake crumbs and hazelnuts.

Beat egg yolks, sugar and vanilla together in another bowl until thick and creamy. Stir in lemon rind, orange rind and combined coffee and water. Fold egg yolk mixture into flour mixture gradually; not all at once.

Whisk egg whites in a clean polished bowl until soft peaks form; fold lightly into pudding mixture.

Spoon mixture into the prepared moulds. Place the moulds in a baking dish; pour in enough hot water to reach halfway up the side of the moulds.

Bake in a moderate oven/180°C for around 35 minutes or until firm to the touch.

Coffee Liqueur Cream Sauce

½ cup fresh or thickened cream

½ cup sour cream

2 teaspoons light brown sugar

1 teaspoon vanilla essence

1 tablespoon Kahlua

1 teaspoon each grated lemon
and orange rind

Combine all ingredients in a saucepan and stir over a medium heat until smooth.

Turn puddings out onto attractive individual dessert plates. Spoon the Coffee Liqueur Cream Sauce over and sprinkle with ground hazelnuts.

SERVES 6

June is at a close, we are well into mustering, it is the middle of winter and the weather is delightful. We have cold nights of snuggling under doonas, followed by clear cool days, warming to 22° by mid-afternoon. Friends and visitors living down south start their exodus north; long journeys in search of the sun.

Leaving behind the terrible winter, they head for clear blue skies that stretch forever over the horizon. The magical days of the north; days of warm sun and endless blue skies, days that only the outback can produce in June and July.

July

Hot Beef Curry with Beer

～

Spaghetti with Walnut Sauce

～

Glazed Beef Ribs, Baked or Barbecued

～

Homemade Sausages

～

Fran's Six-Week Muffin Mix

～

Wild Berry Shortcake

～

Charlie's Laced Coffee

～

My Chilled Coffee Velvet

～

After six weeks of clear days and cold nights, it is difficult to remember the heat of the rainy season. Winter has settled in, so hot spicy food is well and truly the order of the day.

I can never think of hot and spicy without it bringing back memories of my sister and her first attempts at cooking, at least forty years ago. She couldn't cook, but was newly married and so expected to learn how. Like all men, her husband liked his food and his favourite recipe was Hungarian goulash so Susan decided she would tackle this. It was a complete disaster, so bad that even the dogs wouldn't touch the finished product.

Susan followed the recipe 'to the word' but the meat was so tough and hot it burnt your mouth. We went through the recipe together; she had used a good cut of meat and the correct cooking procedure was followed. I couldn't see how she finished with such a result.

I asked again, if she changed anything at all.

'Well,' she replied, 'I didn't have any paprika, so I used this – it's the same colour.' Susan handed me a jar of red pepper. She had added a tablespoon of red pepper to the goulash before serving, to give it a nice colour.

I don't think goulash was ever attempted again, but to this day Susan knows there is a difference between paprika and red pepper, even though they are the same colour!

So remember the red pepper story when you are adding the chilli and curry in the following recipe.

Hot Beef Curry with Beer

This is a hot curry. If you would like it milder, reduce the curry powder and chilli powder.

1 kg topside or round beef steak

½ cup olive oil

2 large onions, chopped

2 tablespoons curry powder

2 tablespoons chilli powder

2 large tomatoes, chopped

2 cups beer

1 tablespoon malt vinegar

½ cup fresh grated coconut

½ cup water

1 teaspoon salt

1 cup canned coconut milk

½ cup fresh chopped parsley

Trim all visible fat from the beef; cut into 2.5 cm cubes. Heat oil in a large frying pan and brown beef well in 3 to 4 batches. Remove from pan and set aside.

Add onions to pan and cook on a medium heat until soft, about 3 minutes. Stir in curry powder and chilli powder and cook, stirring constantly, for another 2 minutes. Add tomatoes, stir well and simmer for 2 minutes.

Add beef, beer, vinegar, coconut, water and salt. Bring to the boil, stirring, then simmer gently, uncovered, for 30 minutes. Stir in the coconut milk and chopped parsley. Cover and cook until beef is tender, about a further 15–30 minutes.

Serve curry with rice and curry accompaniments, such as bowls of chopped tomatoes, spring onions/shallots, bananas, cucumber, mango chutney, shredded coconut, pappadums and lots of cold beer to drink.

Serves 6

Mornings are so cold I sit huddled in a large chair, with hands wrapped around the hot coffee mug to warm my fingers, waiting and watching as the sun slowly creeps into my day. As the sun breaks clear over the mountain range it gradually highlights a spider web. Sunlight shimmers on a single strand of silk that anchors the vast web, as the slightest breath of air moves the web in the cold, still morning. Flickers of light move up and down the strands, highlighting glistening dewdrops.

Finally, the whole web is alight as the sun moves further into the valley and envelops me in a blanket of warmth.

The kitchen calls. The morning is spent making cakes, biscuits, puddings and an endless supply of food required to 'go bush'. Suddenly, the morning has vanished and it's time for a quick and easy, but filling, lunch.

Spaghetti with Walnut Sauce

Walnut Sauce:

100 g walnuts

50 g pinenuts

80 g butter

60 g parmesan cheese, freshly grated

2 cloves garlic, crushed

30 basil leaves, finely chopped

salt and pepper to taste

olive oil as required

Spaghetti

400 g spaghetti

80 g butter

80 g parmesan cheese, freshly grated

To make Walnut Sauce: Using a food processor, mix the walnuts and pinenuts until finely ground. In a saucepan, heat the butter until it foams and turns golden brown. Add the ground nuts; stir for a few seconds. Remove from heat and add cheese, garlic, basil and salt and pepper to taste. Now gradually add a small quantity of hot water and a little olive oil, and mix well until you have a coating consistency sauce. Keep warm.

Meanwhile, cook the spaghetti in a large pan in plenty of boiling salted water until tender, about 10 minutes. Drain well, return to pan and mix with the butter and cheese. Add the sauce and stir gently to coat the spaghetti. Serve immediately, accompanied with a green salad.

SERVES 4

Opposite: Sara relaxing in front of the fire with Charlie's Laced Coffee (recipe page 146). Following pages: Sara, Marlee and Ben, enjoying a barbecue by the pool. Glazed Beef Ribs, Baked or Barbecued (recipe page 137) with salads and Fresh Figs and Fruit Dessert (recipe page 182).

Beef rib bones are so typical of the Australian bush, yet the sight of them brings back to me memories of America, every time. At one of our very first meals in Maryland, sitting in the stately dining room at Lloyds Landing, surrounded by old silver, beautiful crystal and sumptuous food, Marlee's grandmother asked her what Mummy cooked for her on the station. The sincere reply was, 'Bones'.

Over the years, 'Bullo Bones' have progressed!

Glazed Beef Ribs, Baked or Barbecued

2 kg beef ribs, cut into serving size portions

Marinade:

1 cup light or reduced-salt soy sauce

1 cup dry sherry or red wine

6 large cloves garlic, crushed

¼ cup tomato sauce

1 piece ginger 2.5 cm square, finely chopped or grated

½ cup brown sugar or honey or maple syrup

rind and juice of 1 lemon

1 tablespoon French mustard

(If you like it hot, add 1 tablespoon fresh minced chilli)

Trim all visible fat from the beef ribs. Add sufficient water to cover the ribs to boil in a large pan or boiler; add the ribs and simmer gently for 15 minutes. Drain well.

To make Marinade: Place all ingredients in a bowl and mix well.

Pour marinade into a shallow dish; add ribs and turn to coat. Cover and marinate in the refrigerator for 2 hours.

Bake the ribs slowly in a slow oven/150°C for 1 hour or until tender, then brown under the grill for a few minutes. Or barbecue the ribs on a metal hot plate over hot coals. Whether baking or barbecuing, spoon marinade over the ribs frequently during cooking.

Serve with wild rice or jacket-baked potatoes and salad.

SERVES 4 – 6

Opposite: Wild Berry Shortcake (recipe page 144).

Maryland was a food awakening for me. I was never really exposed to truly exotic food until we lived there. In the Philippines, we were warned so often about disease that no-one dared eat anything except the food the American ships brought over from America. So I dutifully did as I was told and stuck to the tried and true recipes that I had grown up with. The eighteen months in between living in the Far East and going to America, we were living on the station and I was in constant shock and not the least bit creative.

In America I suddenly discovered supermarkets so big I got lost just walking around them. They held a quantity and range of foods that I had never dreamed possible. Most of the processed food was either unseen or unheard of in Australia in the sixties.

In 1966 I went into a world of food technology that was difficult to comprehend after living in outback Australia. I started at open freezer displays of frozen bread. The instructions read: 'just put in oven half an hour before serving for piping hot fresh bread'.

Row after row of freezers were filled with every type of frozen food imaginable. Think of a food — it was frozen, even frozen chocolate eclairs! The frozen TV dinners fascinated me the most. I could spend hours in the freezer section just reading the menu listed on each packet.

I don't think these meals ever became as popular in Australia, but in sixties America they were all the rage. The checkout area of the supermarket would be a sea of silver foil trays. The whole meal was in a shallow foil tray and each food had its own little compartment. Even a dessert was attached. If the dessert did not require heating, you tore along a perforated line and that section came away, while the rest went in the oven. If the dessert needed heating, in went the whole tray.

I finally couldn't resist any longer. Each week, dozens of women went by me with these things piled high in their shopping trolleys. I had to try one!

I decided on a turkey dinner, complete with gravy, cranberry sauce, baked potato, sweet potato, peas and cauliflower. It was all contained in the four-centimetre deep tray, along with steamed pudding with a rich sauce for dessert.

I followed the cooking instructions and waited. I suppose the only way to describe the meal was that it was 'bland'. Yes, it was edible, not something you would say was awful, but it just had no taste. It looked great, quite inviting really, but you couldn't get past it, it was 'bland'. If you closed your eyes while chewing, you would have no idea what you were eating. So only one TV dinner came into our house during the four years we lived in Maryland.

I was still well and truly a 'beginner' when it came to cooking, so any major cooking event I tried was accompanied with lots of panic and problems. A dinner party would have me recovering for days, such was the trauma.

Yet I would go to some dinner parties where the hostess would be cool, calm and collected. One woman in particular had me in turmoil. Twenty or so people mingled in her large living room, sipping elaborate drinks and nibbling on complicated appetisers and dips, in endless varieties, yet she never seemed to go into the kitchen and only disappeared a few minutes before dinner was served.

I sat down amazed; there in front of me was a carved baked roast lamb dinner with all the trimmings! How did she do it?

It would have taken me fifteen minutes just to carve the meat! One mouthful gave me the answer. The meat was perfectly carved, in exact proportions and everything was symmetrical! Good heavens, I realised with a jolt, it's a TV dinner! She had served her guests TV dinners – I almost laughed out loud.

Dessert, equally attractive but with no taste, followed. The whole meal was produced from a packet, jar, tin or foil tray. The drinks were ready mixed from a can, the dips from out of a jar and the bread rolls were frozen! No wonder she was cool and calm, although she probably raised a sweat opening all those TV dinners!

I went away happy. Although I might look less than cool and calm when my food hit the table, at least it was tasty. I found out over the years that this was far from an isolated incident. Once, when Marlee had a little school friend staying for the weekend I was cooking chips and hamburgers with salad for their lunch.

She wanted to know what I was doing, as she watched me peel the potatoes. At six years of age she didn't know what a potato was! She had only ever seen frozen French fries in a plastic bag. She didn't know the French fries started out as potatoes.

And it was the same with the beef hamburgers. She had only ever seen them as frozen flat circles in between strips of paper, that lived in the freezer. How they got there and what they were made of, she had no idea. They were simply called burgers.

The little girl couldn't wait to come back to our house and spent the whole weekend peering over the top of the table asking questions. Up to that point in her life, she thought all food came out of the double door freezer in their kitchen, either in a plastic bag or a foil tray. Fresh food was a new and wonderful concept for her.

But of course not all households lived on frozen fare. People on the land lived almost entirely on fresh food, usually created by their own hand.

Mrs Henderson, along with most of the farmers in the district, would every year 'put up' a pig. Hams were smoked using a recipe that went back over one hundred years and sausage was made.

My first year in Maryland I offered to help and was assigned to the sausage making. I soon found out why. The rest of the 'pig processing' was over in a matter of hours, but the sausage process went on and on.

A few hundred kilograms of meat, fat and seasoning had to be put through the mincer three times – Mrs Henderson liked her sausage meat fine! After three times through the mincer it was just like paste. When we finished, I washed my hands to discover that after four hours of seasoning the skin up to my wrists had been bleached whiter than white. My hands were pure white and silky smooth for the next week or so.

I often wonder what happens to your digestive system when this concoction hits it. Although it had an amazing effect on my skin, the recipe is at least free of chemicals – I don't think the same can be said about commercial sausages.

Start with the following recipe and branch out from there; who knows where it may lead.

Homemade Sausages

From America.

500 g lean pork shoulder, finely minced

250 g bacon, rind removed and finely minced

250 g lean beef, finely minced

1 clove garlic, crushed

¼ teaspoon onion salt

¼ teaspoon salt

½ teaspoon cracked black peppercorns

½ teaspoon dried sage

¼ teaspoon ground cloves

¼ teaspoon ground mace

2 tablespoons chopped fresh parsley

1 bay leaf, crushed

pinch of ground allspice

Use a food processor to mince the pork, bacon and beef to a fine 'mince' texture. Add all the remaining ingredients and mix very well.

Place mixture in a bowl or refrigerator container, cover and let it sit in the refrigerator for 24 hours to develop flavour. The mixture may be frozen, at this stage, for up to 3 months.

Mould and roll mixture into sausage shapes or just make into patties, with cold hands.

Heat a heavy-based frying pan over a medium–high heat. Brush pan with a little olive or canola oil. Add 'sausages' or patties and cook until sealed underneath, about 1 to 2 minutes; turn over and cook until other side is sealed. Reduce heat to medium–low and cook, turning occasionally, until cooked through, about a further 10 minutes.

Serve immediately with apple sauce, creamy mashed potatoes or new potatoes and a green vegetable.

SERVES 6

With never enough time to do all that is required and the unexpected always happening on the station, I find the following recipe one of the lifesavers I always fall back on. The fact that the mixture can be kept in the fridge for six weeks means that we can instantly put the mixture into muffin tins and have a batch of fresh muffins in fifteen minutes — invaluable to our hectic lifestyle on Bullo.

Fran's Six-Week Muffin Mix

1 x 425 g packet 'All-Bran' cereal

375 g mixed dried fruits

½ cup chopped pitted dates

3 cups white sugar

5 cups plain flour, sifted

5 teaspoons bicarbonate of soda, sifted

1 cup vegetable oil, canola or macadamia

4 large eggs, beaten

2¾ cups milk

1¼ cups buttermilk

Place 'All-Bran', mixed dried fruits, dates, sugar, flour and bicarbonate of soda in a large mixing bowl. Mix well. Make a hollow in the centre.

Add oil, eggs, milk and buttermilk to centre of bowl and mix well, with a wooden spoon, until evenly combined.

Spoon mixture into greased or paper cup-lined muffin tins, filling muffin cups three-quarters full.

Bake in a hot oven/200°C for 15 minutes, then reduce to moderate/180°C and bake for a further 5 to 10 minutes, depending on muffin size.

Store the remainder of the mixture, tightly covered with clear plastic wrap, in the refrigerator, ready for use when a quick batch of hot muffins is needed.

Do not stir the mixture ever again.

MAKES 48 APPROXIMATELY

One of the cooks who actually stayed for a few months had difficulties, not because she could not learn, but because of the language. She was Dutch and was fairly good at making herself understood, but it soon became apparent that cooking terms, names of spices, foods and cooking utensils are quite different. Not knowing the English word for what she wanted, she asked me one day, 'I need a "water goes, spaghetti stays" please.'

I handed her the colander.

That was over ten years ago and still today whenever I look at a colander that line goes through my mind.

Marlee was one day teaching her how to make paté and after working through the entire procedure she asked if the girl had any questions.

She replied, 'Yes, what does "stew" mean?' She had never heard of a baked dinner and she cooked the roast chicken upside down.

We all persevered and by the end of the month we had a reasonable cook! But Marlee and I still had to tackle the more involved desserts, such as our Wild Berry Shortcake.

Wild Berry Shortcake

2 cups plain flour
2 teaspoons baking powder
⅓ cup caster sugar
40 g unsalted butter, softened
150 ml milk
2 egg yolks, lightly beaten
200 g blueberries
200 g strawberries
200 g boysenberries
200 g raspberries
icing sugar to taste
4 tablespoons raspberry jam
300 ml thickened cream,
whipped

Purée:
¼ cup cranberry juice
¼ cup orange juice
1 punnet strawberries
1 punnet raspberries
4 tablespoons Grand Marnier
2 tablespoons caster sugar
5 tablespoons raspberry jam
3 tablespoons lemon juice

Sift flour and baking powder into a mixing bowl. Stir in caster sugar. Add butter and mix in with a fork to a crumb texture. Add milk and egg yolks, a little at a time, stirring constantly until mixture holds together but is still a soft dough. This is like a scone mixture, so handle as little as possible.

Turn dough out on a lightly floured surface and roll out gently to a fat cylinder shape. Divide in half and pat into 2 equal-sized rounds. Place on a greased baking tray and bake in a hot oven/220°C for about 20 minutes, or until golden brown.

Allow to cool slightly then cut each cake across horizontally to give 4 thin layers. Set aside while preparing the purée.

To make purée: Place all purée ingredients into a blender or food processor. Mix to a purée.

Combine blueberries, strawberries, boysenberries and raspberries in a bowl. Mix gently and add icing sugar to taste. Divide mixed berries, jam, cream and purée into 4 equal amounts.

To assemble the shortcake, place bottom layer on a serving plate; spread witha quarter of jam, then a quarter of the berries and some of the cream, then some purée. Place on the second layer and repeat, and so on. On the top of the shortcake, spread the last of the jam; spoon over the last of the purée and top with the remaining cream and berries.

Serve immediately, or refrigerate until ready to serve.

SERVES 12

It was Charlie's very favourite food – well, all food was favourite to Charlie, but if I cooked this I could get anything out of him! A good main course was the lead-up, followed by 'laced' coffee, a bottle of good port within reach and loud classical music. The shortcake was regally presented and I would quietly whisper my request. Worked almost every time.

The food that really brings back memories of Charlie, however, is his laced coffee. It is especially remembered by the many, many people that he successfully made drunk at breakfast, over the years.

An endless list of unsuspecting pilots have been temporarily grounded after indulging in what they thought was an ordinary cup of 'wake-up' coffee. Most of them not only woke up, they hit the roof when, after many phone calls, they realised they were grounded for the next several hours, if not the day!

I was forever rescuing unsuspecting pilots from Charlie. If I didn't remember to tell them the night before, early morning would find me dashing through the house to the kitchen, at top speed, screaming at the top of my lungs, 'Don't drink the coffee!'

Of course it was all fun and games to Charlie, but back in those days, I was almost always in between cooks, which meant I was cooking most of the time. So Charlie would just disappear into his office, or into his plane and fly away, leaving me to deal with the dismayed, but eventually angry, pilot.

One very funny story was not about the pilot, but the VIP he was flying. They stayed overnight and Charlie, as usual, served him the coffee next morning.

I slept in a few minutes longer thinking everything was okay because the pilot had been 'fully briefed' by me the night before. He was so much 'on the alert' that nothing but water passed his lips, but Charlie managed to sink his boss. After many cups of the lethal brew, the VIP staggered, in a semi-dignified manner, out the door on the opposite side of the house to the airstrip and the plane and exclaimed in a slurred horror, 'Good God! Someone's stolen the aircraft.'

The pilot, having been on pure water for forty-eight hours, was very quick on the uptake.

'No, sir. I parked it on the other side of the house.'

As the pilot and the VIP made their way to the plane the VIP could be heard berating the pilot for doing such a stupid thing as parking the plane on the wrong side of the house!

Most young pilots in the north, and indeed from much further afield, soon learned about Charlie's coffee, or just about Charlie in general. They were always on tenterhooks the entire time they were at Bullo.

Some went so far as to bring their own water, a few even brought survival rations, explaining nervously that they were in training.

One guy even stood guard and slept in the plane, just in case Charlie decided to expand his field of fun.

Now and then a lighter rum version of Charlie's Laced Coffee is a pleasant ending to a meal with friends, and you can tell them about Charlie, or how the pilots of the north survived him. I've provided the recipe with the ratio of rum to coffee that Charlie liked, but adjust the rum according your own taste and stamina!

Charlie's Laced Coffee

¼ cup freshly made good plunger coffee

½ cup Bundaberg rum

¼ cup cream

2 teaspoons brown sugar or raw sugar

and a day to spare!

Mix coffee with rum, cream and sugar in a heat-proof glass or mug. Stir well. Serve immediately.

SERVES 1

If you would prefer something less alcoholic, my Chilled Coffee Velvet is a wonderful way to have your coffee cold and sweet, without the side effects of Charlie's 'laced coffee'!

My Chilled Coffee Velvet

1 egg

1 tablespoon caster sugar

1 cup freshly made fairly strong top quality coffee

½ teaspoon vanilla flavouring essence or 1 vanilla bean, split lengthways

½ cup whipped cream

Beat egg and sugar together in a small bowl until creamy. Pour hot coffee carefully onto the egg and sugar. Stir well. Place mixture in the top of a double saucepan. Stir over gently boiling water until thickened, then allow to cool. Add vanilla and whipped cream. Pour into a jug, cover and chill.

Serve in a tall chilled glass; sprinkle with a touch of nutmeg and cinnamon. If mixture is too thick, stir in extra chilled coffee until the drink is of the right consistency. Serve immediately.

SERVES 1

August

Roast Beef

~

Apple and Almond Pancakes

~

Nutmeg Sauce

~

Stir-Fry Steak and Vegetables, Marlee-Style

~

Bullo Beef Shank and Vegetable Soup

~

Steak and Kidney with Potato Topping or Pastry Caps

~

Korean Steamed Dumplings

~

Sesame Seed Dip

~

Vinegar and Soy Dip

~

Bullo Pizza

~

Bullo Banana Cake

~

Hazelnut Mock Cream

~

Lemon Icing

~

In my early days of learning to cook, tackling a baked dinner was as probable to me as flying to Mars. Having watched my Mum collapse into a swoon every Sunday afternoon from the trials of putting a baked roast dinner on the table, I ruled this dish out of my repertoire as just impossibly hard. Then when I arrived on Bullo and realised I had nothing but beef, I knew I had to conquer this 'baked dinner' thing.

With cookbook in hand I faced the foe and I couldn't believe how easy it was. I worried until the meal was on the table, but everyone was eating with gusto, saying how delicious it was! From then on, it was baked dinners all the way. I could throw a nine kilogram lump of meat in the oven, look at it a few times during the cooking, add lots of vegetables near the end of the cooking and end up carving a lovely juicy, rare slice of beef that made you glad you made it through the day.

Of course, that was after I had conquered the dreaded wood stove. As I already said, I was a beginner when it came to wood stoves. I had no idea that cooking was achieved by hot air circulating around the oven. If ashes were not cleaned out of a little hole at the bottom of the stove, the hot air stopped circulating and nothing cooked. I struggled with that stove until one morning I found Mary cleaning out the ashes and it all became clear why one day it would take hours to cook a roast and then the very next day the same size roast would be burnt to a cinder in half the time. Mary would have cleared out the ashes between the two cookings.

Opposite: Homemade Sausages (recipe page 141).

Roast Beef

Rolled sirloin, corner of topside, round or blade of beef are all tasty cuts to roast, and, of course, the good old rolled rib.

2 – 2.5 kg topside, rolled sirloin, round, blade or rolled rib of beef

1 tablespoon olive oil

250 g medium-size mushroom cups

1 clove garlic, crushed

10 peppercorns

1 bay leaf

pinch of salt

4 tablespoons plain flour

1 cup beef stock

1 cup red wine

½ cup water

2 tablespoons redcurrant or mint jelly

chopped parsley

Brush beef all over with oil, place in a roasting pan.

Roast for the first 20 minutes in a very hot oven/ 230°C, then reduce the heat to 180°C and cook for a further 50 minutes. Add mushrooms to pan, around the beef, and cook for a further 20 minutes. The beef should be nicely cooked at this stage, depending on how you like your beef. Roast it longer if you like it 'well-done'.

Place beef and mushrooms on a serving platter; keep warm while you make a gravy with the meat juices in the pan.

Drain fat from pan juices and leave 2 tablespoons in the roasting pan. Place pan over a medium heat, add garlic, peppercorns, bay leaf and salt; stir for 1 minute. Remove bay leaf and peppercorns. Sprinkle flour over fat; stir constantly over heat for a further 2 minutes, until nicely browned. Gradually stir in stock, wine and water and cook until gravy boils and thickens. Add redcurrant or mint jelly, stir until dissolved. Serve gravy in a sauceboat or jug.

Carve beef at the table and serve with gravy. Our favourite accompaniments are roast potatoes, sweet potatoes, onion, pumpkin, carrots and green vegetables.

SERVES 8 – 10

Opposite: Roast Beef (recipe this page).

Most people long for a family atmosphere in their lives. To sit down to a good meal with family, friends or workmates, gives a belonging to the soul. A lot of the people with problems are 'lonely' people. People just like company and what better place than around a table, with good healthy food, friends, conversation and a sense of belonging.

We seem to have lost this special part of our lives, with the pressures of increased living pace, fast foods and the struggle to survive. No matter how busy you are, stop and join people around a table. Eat healthy, homemade food, talk and sit back and watch how things improve.

When it is someone's birthday on Bullo, no matter how busy we are we always find time for a nice dinner, with a special dish, wine and a birthday cake. Pressures sometimes make it impossible for anything other than the regular meal, but there is always wine and birthday cake.

The celebration means so much to everyone, so we always try to make a special effort and have been rewarded by the wonderful response. I am amazed at the number of people who say they have never had a birthday cake since they were little children – this is sad. But when they have a birthday on Bullo it is always happy.

The following recipe is a favourite birthday dessert.

Apple and Almond Pancakes

1 cup plain flour

2 eggs

¾ cup milk

1 tablespoon grated apple

1 tablespoon ground almonds

pinch of ground nutmeg

extra ground nutmeg and honey for serving

icing sugar and chopped almonds for sprinkling

Pancake mix is always better if left standing for half an hour, so make first. Sift flour into a mixing bowl, add eggs and beat with a wooden spoon until mixture is free of lumps. Gradually add milk, beating constantly to make a smooth batter. Lastly mix in the apple, almonds and nutmeg.

Pour batter into a jug, cover and let stand while cooking the filling.

Filling:

4 cooking apples, peeled, cored and thinly sliced

¼ cup brown sugar

½ cup seedless raisins

grated rind and juice of 1 lemon

1½ teaspoons ground cinnamon

½ teaspoon ground nutmeg

4 cloves

1 tablespoon unsalted butter

½ cup chopped blanched almonds

Filling: Place apples in a medium pan with water to cover, about 1 or 2 cups. Add sugar, raisins, lemon rind and juice, cinnamon, nutmeg and cloves. Bring to the boil, reduce heat and stew, covered, for 4 minutes. Reduce heat to low, add almonds and stew until apples are tender, about 10 minutes. Add butter and let melt through the apples. Remove cloves; keep filling warm.

To cook pancakes: Heat a medium frying pan over a medium-high heat; add a small knob of butter and swirl around the pan covering the whole base well.

Spoon 2 tablespoons of batter into the pan, and swirl around to cover the base. Cook until the underside is golden brown and bubbles appear on top; turn over and cook until other side is golden and cooked.

Transfer pancake to a plate. Continue to make the rest of the pancakes and stack them with a strip of grease-proof paper or foil in between each one. Keep warm.

When ready to serve, sprinkle each pancake with ground nutmeg; spread with a little honey and spoon some apple filling on top, dividing evenly. Roll up the pancakes. Serve sprinkled with icing sugar and almonds. Accompany with Nutmeg Sauce if liked.

SERVES 6 – 8

Nutmeg Sauce

½ cup white sugar

2 teaspoons cornflour

1 cup boiling water

1 teaspoon grated lemon rind

1 tablespoon fresh lemon juice

1 tablespoon unsalted butter

½ teaspoon ground nutmeg

Mix the sugar and cornflour together in a saucepan. Gradually stir in the boiling water. Add the lemon rind and lemon juice and boil for 3 to 4 minutes, stirring constantly. Remove from heat and stir in the butter and nutmeg

Serve sauce warm over Apple and Almond Pancakes.

Variety is often hard to achieve at Bullo and we sometimes have to try food from many different cultures and countries to keep a change on the menu.

When people are isolated in the bush, so far from civilisation, they miss the food halls of the cities that present them with a choice of twenty dishes from many different countries, all under the one roof.

Stir-fries are a great way to get non-vegetable eaters to eat vegetables. They are also very healthy and tasty. Don't follow the recipe too exactly, just use it as a guide. We follow the recipe below substituting whatever vegetables we have at Bullo.

Stir-Fry Steak and Vegetables, Marlee-Style

1 kg beef rump steak, trimmed and sliced into thin strips

1 piece fresh ginger, 2.5 cm square, thinly shredded

4 large cloves garlic, crushed

½ teaspoon sesame oil

2 tablespoons black bean sauce

2 tablespoons cornflour

1 tablespoon white sugar

½ cup light or reduced-salt soy sauce

1 cup dry sherry

3 tablespoons peanut oil

2 large onions, cut into 12 wedges

¼ head broccoli, flower cut into florets, stalk thinly sliced

In a mixing bowl, combine ginger, garlic, sesame oil, black bean sauce, cornflour, sugar, soy sauce and sherry. Mix well. Add steak strips; toss gently until evenly coated.

In a wok, heat 2 teaspoons oil until hot, add one-third of the steak and stir-fry over a medium-high heat until it browns well. Too much meat in the wok will make it mushy and it will not have a good colour. Set steak aside on a plate. Stir-fry remaining steak in 2 batches as directed, using 2 teaspoons oil per batch, and add to meat on plate. Keep hot. Clean wok with paper towels.

Heat remaining oil in wok over a medium-high heat; add onion and stir-fry for 4 minutes. Add broccoli, cauliflower, red and green capsicum; stir-fry for 5 minutes. Add mushrooms, spring onions, snow peas and cabbage; stir-fry until tender-crisp, about 4 minutes.

¼ head cauliflower, flower cut
into florets, stalk thinly sliced

1 red capsicum, seeded
and sliced

1 green capsicum, seeded and
sliced

15 large mushrooms, sliced

6 spring onions / shallots,
cut in 3 cm lengths

30 snow peas, trimmed

¼ small cabbage, thinly sliced

Return steak to wok and stir-fry until heated through, about 3 minutes.

Serve on a large warm serving platter, surrounded by rice, garnished with finely sliced spring onions or fresh chives.

If you wish to serve the vegetables as a separate dish without the steak, add the following to the wok:

1 cup chicken stock

2 teaspoons cornflour

juice of 1 lemon

1 teaspoon sesame oil

salt and pepper to taste

Toss this mixture through the vegetables for the last 3 minutes before they finish cooking, but make sure you don't overcook so that you keep the vegetables crunchy. All-up cooking time for the vegetables should be about 15 minutes.

SERVES 8

Our 'endless' supply of barra actually does run out in the winter; because the water is so cold the fish are not easy to catch. So during winter months we eat more beef than fish. The next two recipes are delicious and warming ways of cooking beef.

Soup is always welcome in winter, especially a hearty one full of meat and other goodies! The following soup is a meal in itself; big chunks of beef on the bone and a good variety of vegetables. Add to this a few loaves of crunchy hot bread coated with melting butter and it soon puts vital ingredients back into a work-weary body. The pie is a variation on an old classic.

Bullo Beef Shank and Vegetable Soup

1.5 kg beef shanks, sliced
4 cm thick

1 kg pork shanks, sliced
4 cm thick

1 cup plain flour

¼ teaspoon dried mixed herbs

¼ teaspoon salt

freshly ground black pepper

1 teaspoon mustard powder

olive oil for frying

2 tablespoons Worcestershire
sauce

1 cup pearl barley

2 cups beef stock

5 litres water

4 onions, thickly sliced

5 carrots, quartered

2 stalks celery, sliced in
5 cm lengths

1 small turnip, thinly sliced

1 parsnip, thinly sliced

250 g mushrooms, halved

chopped fresh parsley for
garnish

Ask the butcher to slice the shanks. Mix flour, dried mixed herbs, salt, pepper and mustard together in a bowl. Roll the beef and pork shanks in the flour mixture to coat them well.

Heat sufficient oil to cover base of a large, heavy frying pan, over a medium-high heat. Add shanks and cook, turning occasionally, until golden brown on all sides. Drain shanks on paper towels.

Place shanks in a large heavy-based pan, add a good grinding of black pepper, Worcestershire sauce, pearl barley, stock and water. Cover and bring to the boil and simmer, half-covered, for 2 hours. Keep skimming the fat off the top throughout the cooking.

If cooking ahead of time, refrigerate overnight and allow the fat to set on the top; remove and proceed the next day.

Add onions, carrots, celery, turnip and parsnip and cook for a further 25 minutes, then add mushrooms and cook for a further 15 minutes. If not thick enough when you add the mushrooms, make a thin paste with cornflour and water, stir in and cook for the remaining 15 minutes. If too thick, add more beef stock.

Soup is ready when the meat is fork-tender. Remove meat from bone and return to the soup; discard bones.

Serve soup with hot fresh bread or garlic bread and add dumplings if liked.

SERVES 12

Steak and Kidney with Potato Topping or Pastry Caps

500 g topside beef steak

2 beef kidneys

¼ cup cornflour

¼ teaspoon dried mixed herbs

salt and freshly ground black pepper

30 g butter

1 large onion, chopped

1 cup water

1 cup red wine

4 large potatoes, thinly sliced

extra 20 g butter

chopped fresh parsley for garnish

Cut steak into 2.5 cm cubes, trim off all fat. Skin kidneys and cut into 1 cm slices; cut out all the white membrane and cube the slices.

Combine cornflour, mixed herbs and salt and pepper to taste in a bowl. Add steak and kidneys to the seasoned cornflour; mix to coat well.

Heat the butter in a heavy-based frying pan over a medium–high heat. Add the steak and kidneys and cook until nicely browned. Transfer to a large pie dish or baking dish.

Add onions to the pan and cook until soft, stirring frequently. Add water and wine and bring to the boil. Mix the remaining cornflour mixture with enough water to make a paste and stir into the pan. Stir until mixture is smooth and thickened slightly.

Pour onion mixture over the steak and kidneys. Make sure there is not too much liquid. Put a layer of potatoes over the top of the steak and kidney, overlapping the potatoes slightly. Dot extra butter on the potatoes, season with more salt and pepper.

Bake in a moderately hot oven/190°C, for about 1 hour, or until the potatoes are golden brown and cooked. If you wish, pastry can be used instead of potatoes. Cook the steak and kidney in a covered baking dish and bake circles of puff pastry on a baking tray. Serve the steak and kidney topped with pastry hats, sprinkled with chopped parsley, accompanied with freshly cooked vegetables.

SERVES 6

At Bullo, we don't draw on every country in the world, but Chinese, Japanese, Italian, Thai, French and Greek recipes are all normal parts of the menu. Now and then a real outsider finds its way onto our plates.

Korean Steamed Dumplings

Filling:

450 g skinless chicken breast
or thigh fillets

175 g bean sprouts, trimmed

6 cubes firm tofu bean curd,
about 250 g

75 g cooked prawns, peeled
and deveined

2 tablespoons peanut oil

1 tablespoon light or reduced-
salt soy sauce

1 tablespoon sesame oil

pinch of chilli powder

freshly ground black pepper

Dough:

225 g plain flour

125 – 150 ml boiling water,
generous measure

To make Filling: Mince the chicken in a food processor, or chop finely. Rinse the bean sprouts under cold running water, then place in a pan with just enough water to cover. Bring to the boil and cook for 2 minutes. Drain well and chop finely. Simmer the tofu in a little water for 2 minutes. Drain well and cut into 1 cm cubes. Finely chop the prawns.

Heat peanut oil in a heavy-based frying pan and cook the chicken, bean sprouts and tofu over a medium heat for 5 minutes, stirring frequently, or until mixture begins to change colour. Add prawns, soy sauce, sesame oil, chilli powder and pepper to taste. Cook for 1 minute, stirring constantly. Remove from heat and chill until required.

To make Dough: Sift the flour into a mixing bowl. Add the water, a little at a time, and mix to a soft dough. Knead well on a lightly floured surface.

Cut dough into 24 equal pieces and roll each into a 7.5 cm round. Make a slight indent in the centre of each round and place a heaped teaspoon of the prepared filling in centre. Moisten the edges of the round with water. Fold the round in half to form a semi-circular dumpling. Repeat until all rounds and filling are used.

Steam the dumplings for 10 minutes. Serve hot with Sesame Seed Dip and/or Vinegar and Soy Dip.

SERVES 6

Sesame Seed Dip

2 tablespoons sesame seeds

¼ teaspoon salt

1 clove garlic, crushed

3 spring onions/shallots, chopped

¼ teaspoon caster sugar

1 teaspoon 'mien chiang', available from Asian food stores

½ teaspoon cayenne pepper

4 tablespoons light or reduced-salt soy sauce

2 tablespoons rice vinegar, available from Asian food stores

Heat the sesame seeds in an ungreased frying pan over a medium–high heat until they begin to 'jump' and turn brown, then remove from pan and pound with the salt in a mortar with a pestle.

Mix together the sesame seed mixture, garlic, spring onions, sugar, 'mien chiang', cayenne pepper, soy sauce and vinegar.

Serve dip with Korean Steamed Dumplings.

An easier dip ...

Vinegar and Soy Dip

½ cup vinegar

1 tablespoon caster sugar

½ cup light or reduced-salt soy sauce

1½ tablespoons finely chopped pine nuts

Heat the vinegar and sugar gently until the sugar has dissolved.

Add the soy sauce and pour the mixture into 6 small individual dishes. Sprinkle some chopped pine nuts into each dish.

Serve dip with Korean Steamed Dumplings.

Even though these recipes give a special lift to our eating world, we can't serve them too often as they are time-consuming and require someone with a fairly developed knowledge of cooking. This mostly means Marlee, but during the mustering season she never has any spare time, so we fall back on grilled steaks and baked dinners until the pressures ease.

But there is one dish the staff can't get enough of, and that's pizza. As you would realise, all the pizza eaten on Bullo is homemade. Well, that's not exactly true. About twenty years ago I did try frozen pizza and it was the first and last time. I'm sure the product has improved over the years, but once we ventured into making our own, we could never go back to the frozen version. Marlee has perfected a mouth-watering Bullo pizza with a thick crunchy bread crust that is just perfect.

I have seen four pizzas, each the size of a scone tray, eaten at one meal by four men. There is no such thing as leftovers with Bullo pizza.

The girls grew up with the longing to 'dial a pizza' from Bullo. But this was never to be, so as soon as they were old enough they made their own pizza — much better than anything they could buy or 'dial'!

Bullo Pizza

Pizza Crust:

30 g fresh compressed yeast

1 teaspoon caster sugar

1 cup lukewarm water

3 cups plain flour

½ teaspoon salt

4 tablespoons olive oil

Filling 1:

4 tablespoons tomato paste

1 cup already-prepared Bolognaise sauce is the quickest, or …

To make Pizza Crust: Cream (mix) yeast with sugar in a small bowl, add lukewarm water, mix well then let stand in a warm place for 10 minutes, or until bubbles appear on the surface.

Sift flour and salt into a mixing bowl; make a well/hollow in the centre; add oil-and-yeast mixture and mix to a firm dough with a clean hand.

Turn dough onto a lightly floured surface and knead for 15 minutes or until smooth and springy.

Filling 2:

3 tablespoons olive oil

500 g finely minced lean beef

1 onion, finely chopped

2 cloves garlic, crushed

1 x 425 g can whole tomatoes

1 teaspoon dried oregano

1 teaspoon dried basil

2 teaspoons sugar

salt and pepper to taste

¼ cup tomato paste

Topping:

250 g mozzarella cheese, grated

⅓ cup grated parmesan cheese

⅓ cup chopped fresh parsley

1 onion, finely chopped

6 mushrooms, sliced

2 teaspoons snipped fresh chives

½ each green and red capsicum, chopped

3 spring onions/shallots, thinly sliced

6 stuffed olives, sliced

2 tomatoes, cut in thin wedges

(or any combination of vegetables you like)

Place dough in a lightly oiled bowl, cover with clear plastic wrap and a tea towel. Stand in a warm place for 20 minutes, or until dough has doubled in bulk (the weather is the guiding rule here; if winter, you need a longer time).

Punch the dough down, give it a good pounding; divide into two and knead each piece into a ball. Flatten the balls into 2 circles to fit 2 pizza trays, making the dough about 2 cm thick.

Press the centre of the dough down onto each pizza tray and work out towards the edge, so that you end up with the middle of the dough about 1 cm thick and a thick edge around the pizzas.

To make Filling 2: Heat oil in a heavy-based pan, add minced beef and cook until colour changes, on a medium–high heat. Remove from pan and cook onions until transparent, stirring occasionally. Add garlic and stir for 1 minute.

Return mince to pan, add tomatoes and juice and all the remaining ingredients, except tomato paste. Bring to the boil, reduce heat and simmer for 25 minutes, until sauce is thick. Cool.

To finish Pizzas: Spread tomato paste over each pizza; divide the Bolognaise sauce or mince filling mixture and spread over tomato paste. Top with half the grated cheeses. Arrange all the other topping ingredients in an attractive pattern on top; sprinkle with the rest of the cheeses.

Brush the edge of the dough with milk for an attractive golden brown result.

Bake in a hot oven/200°C for 15 minutes, or until the crust is golden brown and the filling and topping are cooked. Serve immediately.

MAKES 2 PIZZAS

I always make a very moist banana cake, after the mess I made of my very first banana cake. I had followed the recipe faithfully and yet I ended up with a cake resembling chaff. I experimented with the ingredients and kept making cakes until I had something I considered a tasty cake. I find in dry climates such as Bullo, the recipes need a lot more liquid.

Bullo banana cake became quite famous with the Army troops practising war games on Bullo. It was not unusual to make three cakes a day, each the size of a large baking dish. This was necessary to keep up the supply to troops, who were supposed to be surviving on Army rations, but who just happened to accidentally come across the homestead and drop in to tell us they were there. They would wait hopefully for us to ask them would they 'like a cup of tea and a slice of fresh banana cake?'

Bullo Banana Cake

125 g butter
¾ cup sugar
2 eggs
4 medium ripe bananas
1 tablespoon lemon juice
2 cups self-raising flour
½ teaspoon bicarbonate of soda
¾ cup milk
2 tablespoons shredded coconut
1 tablespoon finely chopped hazelnuts

Cream butter and sugar in a mixing bowl until light and creamy. Add eggs one at a time; beat well after each addition.

Peel and mash bananas and add lemon juice. Mix well. Add to creamed mixture, beat well.

Fold in sifted flour and bicarbonate of soda alternately with the milk. Gently stir in coconut and hazelnuts.

Spoon mixture evenly into two greased and base-lined 18 cm sandwich cake tins.

Bake in a moderate oven/180°C for 25 to 30 minutes until cooked. Cake is cooked when it is firm to the touch. Turn out onto wire cooling racks and cool.

When cold, sandwich the cakes together with Hazelnut Mock Cream and sift icing sugar over the top or ice with Lemon Icing.

SERVES 8 – 12

Hazelnut Mock Cream

1 tablespoon milk
2 tablespoons water
½ cup white sugar
½ teaspoon gelatine
extra 1 tablespoon water
125 g unsalted butter
½ teaspoon vanilla essence
¼ cup ground hazelnuts

Combine milk, water and sugar in a saucepan and stir over a low heat until sugar dissolves; do not boil.

Add gelatine to extra water, mix well. Add to sugar mixture and stir until dissolved. Cool to lukewarm.

Beat butter and vanilla together in a bowl with an electric mixer until white and fluffy. Gradually beat in cooled sugar mixture until fluffy and quite cold (10 to 15 minutes with an electric mixer). Add ground hazelnuts, mix well. Mixture will thicken on standing.

Lemon Icing

1½ cups icing sugar
5 teaspoons fresh lemon juice

Sift icing sugar into a small mixing bowl. Add lemon juice and mix to a smooth paste. Pour over cake and spread smooth with a round-bladed knife dipped in hot water.

With all the cooking lessons constantly going on around them, my girls all naturally wanted to learn. Danielle started young. Her sisters, being five and seven years older than her, were already good cooks, so she was anxious to catch up.

Her first attempt was caramel dumplings. I was busy, so I just gave her the recipe thinking she couldn't go too wrong.

Well, she didn't wait long enough for the syrup to cool and thicken, so she just kept adding sugar, hoping to rectify the problem. By the time I stopped her, there was quite a lot of sugar in the syrup!

I managed to keep it in liquid form to pour over the dumplings. She was so proud of her first dessert and watched to see that we all ate our share.

We took in a month's sugar supply in one sitting! I am happy to say she improved and was soon turning out wonderful caramel dumplings in a delicious syrup. But it did get to the point where the other family members requested that I hide the recipe.

I guided her onto bigger and better things. Chocolate cake was the next recipe to disappear! Danielle soon became a great cook, who cooked a variety of desserts, so it no longer was necessary to hide recipe cards and books.

But despite the messes and failures along the way, I'm glad that my girls all grew up learning how to cook. It is a skill that they will use for the rest of their lives and hopefully pass on to their children.

September

Opposite: Cioppino (recipe page 181). Following pages: Sara's birthday feast: Marlee's Lemon Chicken (recipe page 174), Marlee's Crêpe Suzette (recipe page 175) and Wild Berry Mousse Cake (recipe page 176).

Marlee's Lemon Chicken

∼

Marlee's Crêpe Suzette

∼

Wild Berry Mousse Cake

∼

Steaks Grand Marnier

∼

Cioppino

∼

Fresh Figs and Fruit Dessert

∼

Hungarian Potatoes

∼

Opposite: Stir-Fry Steak and Vegetables, Marlee-Style (recipe page 156).

September brings my birthday, and with it some very funny memories. When the girls were little, the big event was to cook Charlie's and my birthday cakes. As our birthdays were only two days apart one of the girls would cook their dad's cake, then two days later my birthday cake would be created in fierce competition to his. When the time came, the preparation was mammoth, on the scale of a banquet for twenty. The one who wasn't cooking watched every step and criticised at every opportunity. Danielle, being so young, was allowed to do important things like sprinkle flour into the mixture, on the table, in the cake tins, on the floor, in her hair (and just about anywhere she could manage) before the stressed-out chef of the day stopped her.

It was all so very top secret – from their point of view. If I happened to venture into the kitchen during the afternoon, tablecloths and tea towels descended to shroud the evidence. Chef extraordinaire would stare casually at cobwebs on the ceiling, 'judging' chef would look at horses in the paddock, while Danielle repeatedly asked, 'Why aren't we making Mummy's birthday cake any more?' as a tea towel was casually stuffed in her mouth.

I always prepared the evening meal ahead of time to prevent these upheavals. Charlie's job was to keep me out of the kitchen while this great event took place.

One year, Bon was making my cake, Marlee was supervising her every move and Danielle was on her usual flour spree. I was in the office, pretending I had no idea of what was happening.

With the scene set, the preparations began. At one stage Bon came into the office to ask me what lemon essence was, and did we have any. I told her it was in the cupboard next to the vanilla essence. She screamed back from the kitchen, 'Is it a yellow colour?' and I replied, 'Yes'.

Several minutes later an amazing smell invaded the entire house. Charlie was working hard as usual – lying in bed, reading a novel, eating cheese and crackers and washing it all down with beer. He came out of the bedroom in a rush, 'Good God! What is that smell!'

I looked up and smiled. 'My birthday cake.'

Judging from the overpowering aroma that was wafting from the oven and spreading through the house, Bon had not found the lemon essence, but a bottle of eucalyptus drops instead. Now a cake flavoured with the potent drops was baking in the oven.

It took a lot of fast talking and fancy footwork to prevent hurting a little girl's feelings that night, but after many photographs and heaps of praise, she went to bed happy. Bon, like her sisters, went on to become an excellent cook, so that small slip didn't curtail her cooking progress one bit.

To this day, I still think the grand-daddy of all our birthday stuff-ups has to belong to me.

Charlie's birthday was a few weeks away and he was sailing somewhere on the east coast, between Cairns and Melbourne. It was one of those stages in our marriage where communication was at a zero. We even had silent phone calls, sitting on the phone and saying nothing, waiting for each other to speak, but not hanging up. In short, the situation was not good.

We finally both admitted this was crazy behaviour – we needed to discuss our problems and the station's.

Charlie suggested I fly over to my sister's for a break. He would sail there and we could celebrate our birthdays together and talk. What did I think? Still madly in love at that stage, I romanticised a reunion by the sea, crashing waves on a moonlit beach, wet footprints in the sand, sea breezes ruffling curtains by the bed, cold champagne …

Susan and Ralph were very helpful, doing anything they could do to further this millionth reunion. I arrived a day or so ahead of Charlie and spent a good deal of time in a beauty parlour repairing the damage caused by months of hard work in the outback.

As usual, Charlie was a bit out with his ETA (estimated time of arrival). He sailed the boat from Cairns but battled foul weather all the way. When he was one day overdue I became glued to television and radio weather reports. There were grim gale warnings in force along the entire coast for hundreds of kilometres north of us and Charlie was out there somewhere in the middle of it all. I watched the horizon through binoculars for hours on end until my arms ached. I didn't sleep at night; instead I paced my 'moonlit beach' alone.

I called the coast guard hourly, always receiving the same answer; 'no distress messages received'. The third day, nearly at my wits' end, I answered the phone and a weary Charlie said the boat was moored at the wharf near Bundaberg; could I come and pick him up? I had never heard him sound so tired, even his voice was exhausted.

We came home, Charlie collapsed into bed and within seconds was snoring. I stared at my 'Don Juan of the many bedrooms'. He lay spread out on the bed, six days of ratty beard growth covering his face. His hair, thick with salt water spray, was standing on end. Mouth open, he was snoring loudly and mumbling about sailing. Every so often arms gestured wildly or there were bouts of convulsive twitching.

What lay before me was certainly not in any condition to play a part in the romantic interlude I had in mind. I closed the door on the loud snoring.

He slept all day, appeared for dinner in the same dishevelled state, ate an amazing amount of food while grunting inadequate answers to our thousands of questions, finished eating and went back to bed. I sat with Susan and Ralph for coffee and we laughed about the couple of thousand miles I travelled to this great romantic reunion. I retired to bed to curl up next to the smelly, snoring love of my life and dreamed of what might have been.

The next morning Charlie was almost back to his usual self so with only one day left, I put into motion the plans for the much delayed romantic reunion. I guided him into the bathroom; there on a raised platform in the corner was the spa.

I instructed him to sit in it and adjusted the water to the right temperature. He knew exactly what I was up to, so he sat back, enjoyed himself and made me work.

He wanted to read, so I fetched his current book.

Next he wanted something to drink. I presented a bottle of champagne in an ice bucket.

'Something to eat?' was the next innocent request. I returned with some of his favourite snacks.

There sat the object of my desire, naked in a bubble bath, stuffing himself with cheese, crackers and whatever else he could get his hands on, washing it all down with champagne, while puffing on a cigar and reading a book.

'Love is definitely blind,' I told myself as I looked at Charlie, but nevertheless I started to disrobe.

'You haven't turned on the spa,' he replied as he sat waiting for me. I walked over to the bath and hit the switch!

Amazement was followed by disbelief and then I broke into uproarious laughter. Charlie bit the cigar in half and it disappeared into the bubbles, leaving a stub jutting from his lips. His face was frozen in shock.

The spa had not been used for a long time and when I hit the switch, months of accumulated black slime jetted out and covered Charlie in a stinking, oozing mess.

Alarmed by Charlie's shouts, my hysterical laughter and the terrible groans and screeching coming from the water pipes, Susan rushed in. One look at Charlie and she was soon on the floor with me, weak with laughter.

Charlie rallied – forever the lover of centre stage – and quietly asked, 'Is that it, or is there more to follow?'

I left the next day for the station. The faint smell of putrid water was the last lingering memory I had of our farewell embrace.

Like Mother's Day, my birthday is open season and Marlee prepares delicious meals for me. The following menu is one that I love to eat on my 'go for broke', anything goes food day!

Marlee's Lemon Chicken

Lemon Sauce:

2 tablespoons cornflour

½ cup fresh lemon juice

2 tablespoons honey

2½ tablespoons light brown sugar

1 teaspoon grated ginger

6 cloves garlic, crushed

1¾ cups chicken stock

1 onion, finely chopped or quartered and thinly sliced

1 tablespoon light or reduced-salt soy sauce

Chicken:

4 skinless single chicken breast fillets

½ cup cornflour

¼ cup water

4 egg yolks

salt and black pepper

2 cups fresh breadcrumbs, baked until dry

6 shallots/spring onions, diagonally sliced

6 sprigs fresh parsley, chopped

olive oil or peanut oil for frying

To make Lemon Sauce: (before cooking the chicken). Blend cornflour smoothly with lemon juice in a heavy-based saucepan. Add all the remaining ingredients and bring to the boil, stirring; reduce heat and simmer for 30 minutes.

To make Chicken: Trim chicken breasts and cut into 2.5 cm pieces.

Sift cornflour into a mixing bowl. Add water, egg yolks and salt and pepper to taste, beating well with a wooden spoon. Mix to a smooth batter.

Dip chicken pieces into batter then roll in breadcrumbs until evenly coated.

Heat oil, about 4 tablespoons, in a large, heavy-based frying pan and brown the coated chicken in batches. You may need to add more oil to brown all the chicken. When browned, place chicken pieces in a single layer in a shallow baking dish and cook in a moderate oven/180°C, for 10 minutes, or until cooked through.

Drain chicken on paper towels to soak up all excess oil.

Place chicken on a warm serving platter; coat with lemon sauce, garnish with shallots and chopped parsley. Serve any remaining lemon sauce in a gravy bowl. Serve immediately with rice.

SERVES 4

Marlee's Crêpe Suzette

100 g plain flour
2 large eggs, lightly beaten
150 ml water
150 ml beer

Orange Butter:

50 g unsalted butter
100 g icing sugar, sifted
*2 tablespoons orange brandy
or Cointreau*
grated rind of 2 oranges
*juice of 4 oranges or tangerines
or a mixture of both*
extra icing sugar for sprinkling
*2 tablespoons of brandy for
flambeing*

Sift flour into a mixing bowl, make a well (hollow) in the middle; gradually add eggs, then water and beer, beating with a wooden spoon until a smooth batter forms.

Heat a lightly greased crêpe pan or small frying pan over a medium–high heat. Use unsalted butter or olive oil for greasing the pan. Pour in enough batter to thinly coat the bottom of the pan. The crêpes must be very thin.

Cook only until sealed and lightly golden on one side, could be under a minute. Flip over with a palette knife or toss over and cook the other side until golden, usually will take less time. Slide onto a plate and keep warm. Make crêpes as directed with all the remaining batter. Should make about 12 to 16 crêpes.

To make Orange Butter: Place butter and icing sugar in a mixing bowl and beat until light and creamy. Add orange brandy, orange rind and orange juice. Beat well until light and fluffy.

Spread each warm crêpe with a teaspoon of the orange butter, then add a 'dob' to the centre, fold in half, then in quarters.

Arrange crêpes on a serving platter or on individual dessert plates. Spoon the remaining orange butter on top of the crêpes and let it melt. Sprinkle lightly with icing sugar. At the table, spoon 2 tablespoons warm brandy over the dessert and flame with a long match and serve immediately.

You can cut down on the liquor if it's too much, but this is a great way to end your birthday.

SERVES 4 – 6

As unbelievable as it may seem, the finishing touch to the meal was my birthday cake – although I did have to wait a few hours before I could even look at it!

My sister-in-law, Frances, first made this cake for me and I enjoyed it so much I took the recipe home. I raved about it to Marlee, so she decided to make it for my birthday. I must admit I have changed the filling.

Wild Berry Mouse Cake

1 x 280 g packet sponge cake mix (or homemade sponge if you prefer)

2 large eggs

½ cup water

½ cup strawberry and raspberry jam, mixed

¾ cup White Choc Melts

⅓ cup milk

5 teaspoons gelatine, make the measures well-rounded

1 punnet strawberries, chopped

1 punnet mixed raspberries, gooseberries, boysenberries and blueberries, cut in halves (if out of season use frozen)

2 x 300 ml jars/cartons thickened cream

½ cup caster sugar

150 ml extra cream, whipped and strawberries for decoration

1 x 50 g packet flaked almonds, toasted for decoration

Grease a 22 cm round cake tin; line the base with non-stick baking paper.

Make the sponge mixture with the eggs and water, according to pack directions. Pour mixture into prepared cake tin. Bake in a moderate oven/180°C, for 25 minutes, or until cooked. Turn cake out onto a wire cooling rack to cool.

When cool, cut cake into 3 equal horizontal layers. Wash the cake tin and line the same tin with strong clear plastic wrap, with enough to tie over the top of the cake. Place the bottom layer of the cake in the tin, cut side up; spread with a third of the jam.

Place White Choc Melts and 2 tablespoons milk in a saucepan; stir over a low heat until chocolate is melted.

Pour remaining milk into a small heatproof bowl or enamel mug. Sprinkle gelatine over milk; stand container in a pan of simmering water and stir until gelatine is dissolved. Stir gelatine mixture into chocolate mixture; cool slightly.

Reserve a quarter of the berries. Mix the rest in a blender or food processor until smooth. Transfer to a large bowl, stir in the reserved berries, set aside.

Whip cream until it forms firm peaks. Beat in sugar. Fold cream into berry mixture. Stir chocolate mixture into berry mixture. Cover and refrigerate until slightly thickened.

Pour half the mixture over the cake in the tin. Place second layer of cake on top; spread with another third of the jam; pour remaining berry mixture over, top with the remaining layer of cake. Tie the plastic wrap across the top of the cake to keep the layers in place and refrigerate until filling has set.

Untie plastic wrap, turn cake onto a serving plate, remove wrap. Spread top of cake with remaining jam; decorate the sides with the extra whipped cream and press the almonds onto the cream. On the top, decorate the jam with the whipped cream piped or spooned attractively around the edge of the cake; add strawberries to complete the decoration.

SERVES 8 – 12

September heralds change. It is a very volatile month, with sudden shifts in temperature. There will be days of sudden heat, then a violent swing back to mid-winter, with freezing cold nights. One September we had visitors and their first night was so bitterly cold we ran out of blankets. They went to bed fully clothed, just to stay warm.

Just twenty-four hours later they were collapsing in sweltering heat and being invaded by thousands of mosquitoes. Mosquito nets became precious items, imperative to a good night's sleep. You never know what the next day will bring. We can have the first rain storms of the wet season, or get violent wind storms for the whole month without a drop of rain and no promise of relief on the distant horizon.

We had to entertain a plane load of tourists late one September. The day dawned, promising shocking heat and by nightfall all the insects for the entire rainy season had hatched and were visiting Bullo. These were city people, knowing nothing about the outback. They stood transfixed, watching bugs swarming in the thousands, descending on one candle flame and extinguishing it in seconds. We had to serve dinner for twenty under these conditions!

We parked the two Toyota utes ten metres away, outside the dining room French doors, left the doors closed and served dinner by headlight, not candle light.

The bugs entirely covered the two vehicles: each machine was a humming, moving mass. While bugs of all shapes and sizes executed Kamikaze dives into the headlights' beams, we had dinner in peace. Although Marlee and I did talk the guests through the meal, 'What are we eating now?' became quite the party game!

September's changes are never subtle; we get very clear signals of what's up ahead in the coming months. Gone are the calm, blue skies, the cold mornings, the reliable, pleasant weather. September jolts us into the change about to happen; the start of the new season. We sadly realise the 'dry' has gone and that we are in for the approaching wet season. But it's not all bad – September promises the much needed rain, just around the corner.

Meals have to be flexible. One day it will be soups and stew and cold weather, but the next day is sweltering hot and we feel sick in the stomach at the mention of eating.

Light salads during the day and grilled steak at night is what we crave most. The next recipe is a delicious variation on a plain grilled steak.

Steaks Grand Marnier

6 thick slices fillet steak/tournedos, each enough for one serving

1 tablespoon olive oil

1 clove garlic, crushed

½ teaspoon chopped fresh rosemary

60 g butter

½ cup Grand Marnier

⅓ cup cream

¼ cup chopped fresh parsley

1 tablespoon chopped fresh chives

1 tablespoon chopped fresh mint

salt and freshly ground black pepper

Remove any fat from the steaks and use to grease a heavy-based frying pan. If no fat, grease lightly with olive oil.

Heat pan over a medium–high heat until very hot; add steaks, a few at a time, and seal one side for a few minutes, then turn over and seal other side. Depending on your taste, the steaks should be ready in another few minutes. Only turn steaks once!

If you like your steak on the well-done side, leave it there for a bit longer, on a medium heat.

Remove steak, arrange on a serving platter and keep warm in the oven.

Meanwhile, make the sauce. Reduce heat and, when pan is slightly cooler, add 1 tablespoon oil, garlic and rosemary; cook gently, stirring, for 1 minute. Add butter; stir until melted. Add Grand Marnier; stir until combined, scraping pan juices from the bottom of the pan into the sauce.

Add cream, parsley, chives and mint, bring to boil; reduce heat and simmer, uncovered, for 2 minutes or until sauce thickens slightly. Season to taste with salt and pepper.

Pour sauce over steak and serve with freshly cooked vegetables or salad, or both.

SERVES 6

I was in San Fran a few years ago, twenty years after my first visit, and I was surprised to realise that the differences in both our food preparation and the types of food that we eat are just as marked as they were when I was living there. Australia and America are still worlds apart.

Marlee and I went out for breakfast the first morning. We ordered poached eggs on toast and crispy bacon. A dinner plate was placed in front of us with two very small, thin, crispy strips of bacon, but no toast or eggs. Several small containers, about halfway between an eggcup and a teacup in size, were placed on the table. We asked the waitress where our order of poached eggs on toast was. We were told, in curt tones, that it was in front of us, and that we had to get the toast from the 'serve yourself bar'. We peered cautiously into the little bowls and there in the bottom of each nestled a poached egg.

We dutifully collected the toast, rescued the poached egg from the bowls and assembled our breakfast.

Lunch was more of the same. I have no idea if this is peculiar to San Fran or if it is widespread, but it is a strange way to serve food. I think it is done like this to save them the trouble of waiting on you.

Despite the strange serving customs, this recipe is not bad. It is especially welcome on the occasional September evening when the temperature drops and we are plunged back into winter.

Cioppino

Fish stew from San Francisco. Recipe given to Frances fifteen years ago.

½ cup olive oil

3 cloves garlic, crushed

¾ cup chopped green capsicum

¾ cup chopped spring onions / shallots

2 x 425 g cans tomatoes or 1 kg fresh tomatoes, quartered

¾ cup tomato paste

2 cups white wine

2½ cups water

½ cup chopped fresh parsley

1 tablespoon chopped fresh basil

1½ teaspoons chopped fresh oregano

½ teaspoon salt

¼ teaspoon white pepper

750 g firm-fleshed fish fillets; barramundi, ling or ocean perch

500 g green prawns, peeled and deveined

1 x 250 g can clams or scallops, drained, or 250 g either, fresh

Heat oil in a large heavy-based pan over a medium heat; add garlic, capsicum and spring onions and cook for about 8 minutes, stirring frequently. Add undrained tomatoes, tomato paste, wine, water, parsley, basil, oregano, salt and pepper to pan. Stir well and simmer for 10 minutes, uncovered.

Skin the fish fillets and cut into 2.5 cm square pieces. Add to pan with prawns and clams or scallops. Simmer, covered, for 15 minutes, then uncovered for 10 minutes. Serve with rice and sourdough bread, if you can get it!

SERVES 8

The next recipe also takes me back to America (this time to the east coast) and to lazy summer days and tennis courts surrounded by green lawns right to the river's edge. A sailboat laps gently at the wharf and lunch and drinks are served on the screen porch. It is straight out of the *Great Gatsby* era.

This dessert is quick and simple, and to my mind, quite delicious.

Fresh Figs and Fruit Dessert

10 fresh ripe figs, washed and sliced

4 large bananas, sliced and covered with fresh lemon juice

250 g green grapes, cut in half and seeds removed

light brown sugar for sprinkling

coffee sugar crystals for sprinkling

300 ml fresh or thickened cream, stiffly whipped

Arrange the prepared fruit in circles on a flat serving plate. Cover with clear plastic wrap and chill in the refrigerator.

A few minutes before serving, sprinkle fruit firstly with a hint of brown sugar then with some coffee sugar crystals, just sufficient for the brown sugar to melt and coffee sugar crystals to soften a little but still have some crunch left.

Serve the cream in a small bowl in the centre of the fruit; sprinkle just a hint of each sugar over the cream. Serve immediately.

SERVES 6 – 8

The images connected with this simple dessert are so strong I know they will never fade. Even now as I sit here writing, I can see the setting so clearly: the lovely old home, its history reaching back to the Civil War and further, surrounded by sweeping, lush lawns, bordered with weeping willows. A timelessness hung over that house that drew me back to the nineteenth century.

Another recipe that takes me back in time is Hungarian potatoes. My sister Sue was still learning to cook for her very exacting husband, who would instruct her on how every dish was to be prepared.

I arrived one day to find her in a stew — she had lost the instructions of how to make his favourite potatoes. We couldn't find the piece of paper — even though the house was searched from top to bottom — so we made it up.

He raved about the potatoes and said they were just like Mother cooked. Here is the recipe as Mother *didn't* cook them!.

Hungarian Potatoes

8 medium potatoes

2 onions, finely chopped

½ cup chopped fresh parsley

120 g ham, finely chopped

4 tablespoons French mustard

salt and freshly ground
black pepper

½ cup cream

¼ cup freshly grated parmesan
cheese

extra grated parmesan cheese
and chopped fresh parsley
for sprinkling

Peel and wash the potatoes; grate roughly, not finely. Squeeze out all the juice with clean fingers.

In a bowl, mix the potatoes with onions, parsley, ham, mustard and salt and pepper to taste. Fold in the cream and the cheese.

Spread mixture in the bottom of a large, greased baking dish. Sprinkle with a light touch of grated cheese.

Bake in a moderate oven/180°C, for about 45 minutes or until golden brown and potatoes are cooked. Sprinkle with parsley and serve immediately.

SERVES 6 – 8

The smell of baked potatoes must be one of the most mouth-watering smells there is. Back in the early days on the station, when the cattle work was done on a horse, I was riding home, hanging in the saddle after a long day of mustering. I was saddle-sore, bone-weary, thirsty and hungry – too tired to lift my head. My horse was in the same condition, plodding along, its head relying on its homing instinct to take us home.

Suddenly, my head came up with a jolt. A delicious aroma of baked potatoes was filling my nostrils. But how could it be? I was still a few kilometres away from home, out on a vast empty plain with nothing in sight except for a tree. You've guessed it – the smell of potatoes was coming from the tree.

I rode around the tree sniffing and inhaling this delicious aroma. My horse was pleading to go home – the smell of baking potatoes didn't affect him in the slightest! After a few more deep breaths I headed for home with renewed vigour, just from the smell and the thought of baked potatoes. Such is the power of food.

It's hot, the musters are coming to a close and some of the staff have left.

September leaves me with memories of spas, Charlie and birthdays with a difference.

Opposite: Brownies from the North (recipe page 194) and Brownies from the South (recipe page195).
Following page: Saturday Night Plum Duff (recipe page 198).

October

Wiener Schnitzel

~

Hot Lemon Sauce

~

Maryland Beaten Biscuits

~

Cold Mango Crab

~

Brownies from the North

~

Brownies from the South

~

Bullo River Stockcamp Bread

~

Saturday Night Plum Duff

~

Custard

~

Stockcamp Damper

~

Stockcamp Casserole

~

October has you putting away doonas and warm clothing, accepting without a doubt that the wet season is on its way.

Stockmen wipe their brow every few minutes while working, to keep sweat out of their eyes. Cattle move at a slower pace and by midday they are reluctant to move at all. Men talk of going south, of moving on to cooler weather and the season is just starting.

The last muster is 'bush', over thirty kilometres from the homestead. Marlee has her hands more than full, working short-handed, in increasing heat, struggling with a road churned to 'bull dust' by road trains. Land, equipment, animals and people are all crying out for the 'break', for the rainy season to start.

Even though the next recipe is a favourite of Franz's, we were cooking Schnitzel long before he came into our lives. We love it but nowhere near as much as Franz does.

Wiener Schnitzel

8 large thin veal steaks, allow 1 steak per person, but we find the men always eat at least 2, and more!

4 tablespoons fresh lemon juice

½ cup dry white wine

2 eggs, lightly beaten

½ cup milk

½ cup cornflour

6 tablespoons olive oil

60 g butter

chopped fresh parsley for garnish

lemon wedges for serving

Seasoned Breadcrumbs:

2 teaspoons mustard powder

2 teaspoons grated lemon rind

2 tablespoons chopped fresh parsley

¼ teaspoon freshly ground black pepper

1 cup fresh breadcrumbs

1 cup dry breadcrumbs

Trim skin from the veal steaks to prevent them from curling during cooking. Remove any sinews. Pound the steaks until evenly thin. Place veal in a shallow dish; sprinkle with lemon juice and wine. Cover and marinate for 1 hour.

Meanwhile, prepare seasoned breadcrumbs by mixing all the ingredients together. Place breadcrumb mixture on a sheet of greaseproof paper. Beat eggs with milk; pour into a deep plate or round pie dish.

Dip veal into cornflour, turning to coat; shake off excess. Place veal in egg mixture; coat well, using a pastry brush, then place in Seasoned Breadcrumbs; turn to coat well and press breadcrumbs on firmly with clean fingertips.

Place coated veal on a large tray, in a single layer, and chill for 1 hour before cooking.

Heat 1½ tablespoons oil and a quarter of the butter in a large heavy-based frying pan over a medium–high heat. Add 2 veal steaks and cook for 3 minutes on each side, turning once, or until the crumbs are a good golden brown. Drain on paper towels. Cook the remaining veal in more oil and butter, in batches, as directed.

Serve immediately sprinkled with chopped parsley, accompanied with Hot Lemon Sauce (recipe follows), lemon wedges, potatoes and green vegetables.

Serves 8

Hot Lemon Sauce

2 cups chicken stock
30 g butter
2 tablespoons cornflour
½ cup cold water
4 egg yolks
grated rind and juice of
2 lemons

Heat the chicken stock and butter in a heavy-based saucepan over a medium heat. In a small bowl, blend the cornflour smoothly with the water; stir into the hot stock mixture and bring to the boil, stirring constantly. Simmer for 2 minutes.

In a second bowl, beat together the egg yolks, lemon rind and lemon juice until frothy. Gradually add ½ cup of hot sauce mixture to the egg yolk mixture, stirring constantly. Then pour this mixture back into the rest of the sauce mixture, stirring all the time.

Do not let the sauce boil, as this will curdle the eggs. Keep warm until ready to serve. If liked, you can make this sauce ahead and store it in the refrigerator. It will keep for a few days. Serve with Wiener Schnitzel.

For years before I went to Maryland, Charlie never stopped talking about both Maryland ham and Maryland Beaten Biscuits. So over the years the anticipation grew and when I arrived in Maryland I was finally served Maryland ham and Maryland Beaten Biscuits.

Well, the ham lived up to its reputation, but I really don't know what the raving over the biscuits was about. When I tasted them I was very disappointed and in the four years I lived in Maryland, my opinion didn't change.

Nora, the cook, produced these amazing biscuits and the way most people talked, you would think it was food from the gods. To me, they tasted like a very heavy flour and water mixture that had gone horribly wrong!

This all happened thirty years ago. Now, having just read the recipe again, I wonder even more why anyone would go to all the trouble to produce something so dull and tasteless. Here is the recipe, regardless.

Maryland Beaten Biscuits

1 large sawn-off tree trunk (table height)

1 axe

4 cups all-purpose (plain) flour

1 teaspoon salt

1 tablespoon lard

milk

water

Sift flour with salt and work in lard. Have ready a mug filled with equal parts of milk and water.

Add it gradually to the other ingredients, kneading all the while, stopping as soon as the flour will hold together. For the dough should be very stiff.

Beat for the next 30 minutes with an axe.

Prick with a fork and bake until a delicate white (in a 180°C oven). When they say 'Beaten Biscuit', they mean it; one just wonders, why? A 'modern' version exists; instead of the axe, you put the dough through a meat grinder 5 times. The mind boggles when you think what these biscuits might be called!

However, there is one biscuit that I remember that was pleasant. And, in total contradiction to the above, the advice on cooking these biscuits was 'don't fuss the dough'! Make the dough quickly and get them in the oven straight away.

2 cups all-purpose (plain) flour

4 teaspoons baking powder

1 teaspoon salt

4 tablespoons shortening (butter or margarine)

⅔ cup milk

Sift flour, baking powder and salt into bowl. Cut shortening into mixture until it forms tiny balls.

Add milk and stir quickly with a fork, until you have a soft dough. Knead dough quickly on a floured board.

Pinch off the dough, enough to make small balls. Roll them lightly in your hand and flatten into circles, the dough about 1 cm thick.

Place on cookie (baking) trays and bake at 260°C for 10 minutes, or until cooked.

This is much more pleasant than attacking the poor old dough with an axe for half an hour. But, of course, you wouldn't have to do your aerobics if you made Beaten Biscuits every day!

After the last steer has walked onto the truck, the last road train has closed its gate and Marlee has hauled the road train over the worst sections of our road (so it doesn't bog down in the bull dust) it's finally time to slow down.

We now ready the station for the approaching 'wet'. We collect and put away all the equipment that has been spread over the property during the six months of the dry season. And before the stockcamp depart south to cooler climates, Marlee and I must drive to town to stock up on everything needed to last us through the five months that we are cut off by floodwaters. For about six months of the year, our road is cut by the flooded Bullo River and creeks, making it impossible to reach the front gate.

So, leaving the most reliable stockman in charge, we jump in the truck, drive through the night, hit town at daylight, shop all day until the shops close and then dine out on an extravagant meal, cooked by someone else!

After a few hours' sleep, we leave for home at midnight, arriving back around morning tea time, hoping the place is still in one piece and no 'Uncle Dick' events have happened. Of course I am referring to earlier times, when Marlee and I were battling alone. Now that we have Franz, life is so much easier. With three of us on the station, two can go to town for longer than just an 'overnight dash' and not panic or worry what awaits us when we return.

Seafood, other than barra of course, is always on our minds when we are in town and during the crab season we overindulge. If we are leaving town by plane, we buy wholesale crabs to take home and cook some of our favourite crab recipes. Marlee or Franz attend to the cooking; as I have said previously, if the poor thing is alive, I leave quickly.

I had to smile once while reading about steaming crabs in an old recipe book from America. The warning was, 'Hold the lid down tight. Don't forget, they will bite you if they can!' That's the understatement of the year; if the poor creature is on a rack over boiling hot water, why wouldn't it bite!

We do live in crab country on Bullo. Thick mangrove swamps edge the shores of the Victoria River in our lower paddocks, but there are also some mighty big crocs living there. Franz, being the keen fisherman he is, decided he would trap a few mud crabs. He welded together a massive stainless steel mud crab trap, capable of trapping dozens of crabs in comfort, and set it in the river near the mangroves. The next day Franz rowed out, anxious to see his catch. He pulled into the boat a trap squashed flatter than a pancake, with the couple of kilos of meat bait gone.

Realising the size of jaws needed to squash the trap, Marlee and I begged Franz not to continue trapping for mud crabs. The idea of him out on that river in a small aluminium boat, with something that could squash that massive trap flat, made our blood run cold. I don't think Franz was keen to come face to face with the big croc, either.

So we buy crabs and keep the squashed trap hanging in the workshop, as a reminder to Franz when he gets the urge to go and catch a crab.

Cold Mango Crab

Use half a crab per person as a rough guide. But if you like crab, maybe use a few more.

4 fresh cooked crabs

3 mangoes

1 orange, ½ thinly sliced for garnish, ½ peeled

2 teaspoons chopped fresh mint

1 cooking apple, peeled, cored and grated

1 white heart of celery, thinly sliced

lettuce leaves, chopped parsley, sliced spring onions, julienne strips of lemon and lime rind for serving

Mayonnaise:

1 egg yolk

1 tablespoon Dijon mustard

salt and white pepper

¾ cup chilled olive oil

3 teaspoons fresh lemon juice

Shell crabs, remove crabmeat and set aside.

Cut mangoes in half and scoop out all the flesh into a blender or food processor. Add the peeled half of the orange and the mint and mix well to a puree.

Place the crab in a bowl and carefully fold in the mayonnaise, mango mixture, apple and celery.

Serve in whole lettuce leaves and sprinkle with parsley, spring onions, julienne strips of lemon and lime rind and garnish with orange slices. Serve immediately with crunchy wholemeal bread rolls.

To make Mayonnaise: Beat egg yolk in a bowl with mustard, salt and pepper to taste. Add oil, a drop at a time, beating constantly. As mayonnaise thickens, beat in some of the lemon juice. Continue adding all the oil, slowly, beating constantly. Add more lemon juice and salt and pepper to taste.

SERVES 4 – 8

The two following recipes came from north and south of the Mason-Dixon line (the line that divided America during the Civil War).

Some unusual situations were created when this line cut states in half. Friends and family that only lived across the river from each other suddenly found themselves on different sides, regardless of their ideals, opinions or beliefs. The division and competitiveness created by this imaginary line – drawn in the sand – still exists today, to some extent.

The following two brownie recipes are a reflection of this division and both are deliciously American.

Brownies from the North

250 g unsalted butter
175 g dark cooking chocolate
1½ cups caster sugar
4 large eggs
2 teaspoons vanilla essence
1 cup self-raising flour
1 cup chopped walnuts

Chocolate Icing:

150 g dark cooking chocolate
3 teaspoons unsalted butter
3 tablespoons boiling water

Melt butter and chocolate in the top of a double-boiler, over gently bubbling water, stirring constantly, until smoothly combined.

Beat sugar and eggs together in a mixing bowl until mixture is thick and fluffy.

Fold chocolate mixture into egg mixture. Add vanilla and fold in flour until well combined, then fold in the walnuts.

Pour mixture into a base-lined and well-greased 23 cm square cake tin. Bake in a moderate oven/180°C, for 30 to 35 minutes, until cooked. Test with a fine skewer.

Cool in tin, standing on a wire cooling rack. Ice while still warm; leave in tin until cold, then cut into squares.

To make Chocolate Icing: Place chocolate, butter and water in a heatproof mixing bowl over a pan of barely simmering water until melted and combined. Mix well. Remove from heat; cool to a spreading consistency. Spoon icing over the warm brownies.

MAKES 16

Brownies from the South

Base:

60 g dark cooking chocolate

70 g unsalted butter

½ cup plain flour, sifted

1 cup quick-cooking oats

½ cup firmly packed light brown sugar

⅛ teaspoon bicarbonate of soda

Topping:

90 g cooking chocolate

⅔ cup plain flour

¼ teaspoon baking powder

125 g unsalted butter, softened

¾ cup caster sugar

3 large eggs

1¼ teaspoons vanilla essence

⅔ cup chopped walnuts

Chocolate Icing:

155 g cooking chocolate, coarsely chopped

3 teaspoons unsalted butter

3 tablespoons boiling water

¼ cup walnuts, ground in a blender or food processor

2 tablespoons chopped walnuts for decoration

To make Base: Melt chocolate and butter in the top of a double-boiler, over simmering water; mix well.

In a mixing bowl, combine flour, oats, brown sugar and bicarbonate of soda. Add chocolate mixture; mix well.

Press mixture evenly into a lined and greased 20 cm square cake tin.

Bake in a moderate oven/180°C, for about 15 minutes. Set aside on a wire cooling rack and allow to cool slightly.

To make Topping: Melt chocolate and let cool. In a mixing bowl, sift flour and baking powder; set aside.

Cream together butter and sugar in a second mixing bowl until light and fluffy. Add eggs, one at a time, and beat well. Stir in vanilla essence and the cooled chocolate. Fold in the flour mixture and walnuts.

Spread topping evenly over the partially cooled base. Bake for a further 35 minutes until cooked. Test with a fine skewer. Cool on a wire cooling rack.

To make Chocolate Icing: Combine chocolate, butter and water in a heatproof mixing bowl over a pan of barely simmering water; stir until evenly combined and smooth.

Remove from heat; cool until a spreading consistency and fold in the ground walnuts.

Pour icing over the cooled brownies. Sprinkle chopped walnuts over the icing before it dries. Cover and let stand for several hours before cutting into squares.

MAKES 16

I put in this next recipe, plain bread, in the hope that it will inspire you to try bread making and maybe branch into bigger and better bread recipes. As I have said before, there is nothing like the smell of fresh bread baking. It creates memories that stay with you all your life.

I can still clearly remember my first lesson in bread making with Mary. I was hopeless for a long time, but finally mastered it and produced good bread that didn't turn to a brick once it cooled.

I still have visions of rising dough cascading down the stairs! In the winter I put the bowl of dough (enough for ten loaves) halfway up the stairs, where the morning sun kept it warm and made it rise more quickly. When I had a bad day and had forgotten about the bread, I was jolted back to reality by two little girls running around the tin shed, looking for their mother.

'Come quickly, Mummy,' they would scream, 'the bread is walking down the stairs!'

The forgotten dough would rise and spill over the bowl, then start a journey down the stairs. The worst case found the dough down two steps and hanging over the edge, reaching for the third.

I forgot it so many times I finally spread a clean cloth on the stairs below the bowl to keep the dough clean when it ventured down the stairs.

Bullo River Stockcamp Bread

8 cups plain flour, sifted

1 tablespoon dry instant yeast or 30 g fresh compressed yeast

1 tablespoon white sugar

1 tablespoon salt

60 g butter

approximately 1 litre lukewarm water

In a large mixing bowl, mix together all the dry ingredients, including the instant dry yeast. Make a well (hollow) in the centre and add butter and lukewarm water gradually (melt the butter in the water first to make it easier to mix) and mix to form a dough.

If using fresh compressed yeast, do the following:

Cream the yeast with a teaspoon of sugar; add 1 cup of the lukewarm water and stir until combined; sprinkle

1 tablespoon of flour over the mixture; cover bowl and stand in a warm place for 10 to 15 minutes, or until frothy. Then add to the dry ingredients along with the remaining water and butter; mix to a firm dough. (You will also have to do one extra 40 minutes rising and one extra kneading.)

For both methods, add enough water, approximately 1 litre, to make a good dough – it should stay together, but not stick to the hands. Add more flour if necessary.

Knead mixture in the bowl with one hand until well mixed, turning the bowl with your free hand. Turn out onto a lightly floured surface. Knead the dough well for at least 5 to 10 minutes. Return to the lightly greased or floured bowl and cover. Put in a warm place for 20 to 30 minutes and let rise; it should double in bulk.

Punch dough down in the bowl, turn out onto the floured surface and knead again for 5 minutes.

Make dough into required shapes. For loaves, make into 2 balls of dough and place into two 23 x 12 cm loaf tins. For rolls, knead and form into 20 to 24 small balls of dough, remembering they double in size, and place on a baking tray

Set aside, covered, in a warm place, to prove or rise again for another 15 to 20 minutes. Brush the top of the dough with a mixture of egg yolks and water for a shiny top, or sprinkle with flour for a different finish.

Bake in a very hot oven/230°C, for 5 minutes, then reduce to a moderate oven/180°C, and bake according to size. Loaf, 45 to 50 minutes, or until cooked, rolls, 30 to 35 minutes. To test if bread is cooked, it should make a hollow sound when you knock with a knuckle on the top or bottom.

MAKES 2 LOAVES OR 20-24 ROLLS

In one of my books I wrote about a dessert we had on Saturday night out in the stockcamp, but couldn't remember the name. Judging by the amount of letters I received about this dessert, it is widespread throughout Australia. Readers have provided me with many names, but just the other day I remembered what our old cook called it: 'Plum Duff'.

In the following recipe I have glamorised it, just a bit. The reason it was dumped in hot jam sauce was to hide the taste of melted-down beef fat, which is all they had to cook with back in the early days.

So I have left out the beef, kept the jam sauce and added an extra-rich version of the plain 'bush' custard.

Sit out under the stars to eat this dessert.

Saturday Night Plum Duff

½ quantity Bullo River Stock Camp Bread dough

2 tablespoons white sugar

1 teaspoon grated lemon rind

½ teaspoon ground nutmeg

egg white for glazing

plum and raspberry jam for filling

oil for frying

Coating:

caster sugar

ground cinnamon

grated lemon rind

Sauce:

plum and raspberry jam

At the stage in the breadmaking when you put the dough into the tin, do the following.

With the dough still in the bowl, add white sugar, grated lemon rind and ground nutmeg; knead lightly into the dough.

Roll the dough out on a floured surface to about 1 cm thick. With a floured 5 cm pastry cutter, cut out rounds of dough.

Brush half the rounds of dough with lightly beaten egg white; put 1 teaspoon of plum and raspberry jams, mixed together, in the middle of these rounds. Put the remaining rounds on top of the 'jam rounds' and pinch the edges together firmly.

Cover with a clean tea towel and let rise in a warm place, until double in size.

Shallow fry in batches in a large heavy-based frying pan in enough oil to reach halfway up the side of the dough. Make sure oil is sufficiently hot. Turn once, when underside is golden brown. Cook second side until the same golden brown. Do not let the oil get too hot. Keep it at a constant heat by reducing and increasing the heat during cooking each batch.

Turn plum duffs out onto paper towels and drain well for a minute or so. While still hot, roll in coating.

When ready to serve, drop plum duffs into a saucepan of bubbling hot mixed plum and raspberry jams, for 10 seconds. Serve in bowls; spoon more of the jam on top and surround with custard.

MAKES 12 – 16 APPROXIMATELY

Custard

2 cups milk
3 tablespoons white sugar
4 egg yolks
1 teaspoon rum

In a heavy-based saucepan, over a medium heat, mix milk and sugar and stir until sugar is dissolved and milk is very hot.

In a small bowl, beat the egg yolks lightly, then stir in a few tablespoons of the hot milk mixture. Then return the egg yolk mixture to the hot milk in the saucepan.

Reduce heat to low and cook, stirring constantly, until the mixture thickens, about 5 minutes. Do not boil or custard will curdle.

Remove saucepan from heat and place in a pan of cold water. Continue to stir the custard for another 2 minutes, then stir in the rum.

To make a very rich custard add ½ cup cream, whipped, to the warm custard.

Serve Custard hot with Plum Duff.

During our busiest times in the mustering season, damper is made almost every day. When you 'break camp' daily, moving in search of cattle, you have very little spare time. I knew one old stockcamp cook (who also doubled as the horse tailer) who made bread dough before sunrise when we 'broke camp', put it in a camp oven and tied the lot on top of the mule's pack load to let the dough rise while he walked the horses to the next camp.

He would knock it down during morning smoko, put it back on the mule and head for dinner camp. Once there, he'd knock down the dough the last time, light a fire and bury the camp oven in hot coals. The men, out mustering, were able to find dinner camp just by following the smell.

Those cooks are few and far between, so most of the time we eat damper. Serve it with the Stockcamp Casserole (recipe follows).

Stockcamp Damper

3 cups self-raising flour
1½ teaspoons salt
1 tablespoon powdered milk
90 g butter
½ cup milk
½ cup water
extra milk and flour

Sift flour, salt and powdered milk into a mixing bowl; add butter and rub in until mixture looks like fine breadcrumbs. Make a well in the centre of the flour mixture and add combined milk and water. Mix with a round-bladed knife until a soft dough forms.

Turn dough out onto a lightly floured surface; knead lightly and shape into a round ball. Place on a greased baking tray. Pat the dough out to a 15 cm round.

With a sharp knife, cut across the top of the dough, about 1 cm deep, to cut the damper into quarters, then cut each into wedges. Brush the top with milk and sprinkle a little flour over the milk.

Bake in a hot oven/200°C, for 10 minutes, then reduce to moderate/180°C and bake for a further 15 minutes. Cool on a wire rack but eat warm.

SERVES 8 – 12

Opposite: Franz's favourite, Wiener Schnitzel (recipe page 189). Following pages: Bullo River staples, Stockcamp Casserole (recipe page 201) and Stockcamp Damper (recipe this page).

Stockcamp Casserole

1 kg round or blade or skirt beef steak (I use a combination)

2 tablespoons olive or canola oil

2 onions, coarsely chopped

1 x 450 g can red kidney beans

1 x 450 g can mixed beans

1 x 450 g can tomatoes, cut in half

1 cup water

2 tablespoons golden syrup or brown sugar

2 tablespoons brown or white vinegar

¾ teaspoon freshly ground black pepper

¼ teaspoon salt

good pinch of mixed dried chopped parsley to garnish

Trim beef and cut into 3 cm cubes. Heat oil in a heavy-based frying pan and cook beef in about 3 batches, until lightly browned. Place beef in a camp oven if out bush, or in a large casserole if at home.

Gently fry the onions in the pan, until soft, stirring frequently, about 5 minutes. Add onions to beef, along with beans, tomatoes with liquid, water, golden syrup, vinegar, pepper, salt and mixed dried herbs.

Cover casserole and cook in a moderate oven/180°C, for 1½ hours, adding more liquid if and when necessary. Or simmer over a low heat in a large, covered, heavy-based pan, or cook in a camp oven for 1¼ to 1½ hours, until meat is tender.

Serve sprinkled with parsley, accompanied with damper or fresh bread and lots of potatoes or rice or steamed dumplings.

SERVES 8

Sitting around a camp fire eating damper with a solid meal of beef has always been a part of the Australian bush. Nowadays people from all walks of life go on holiday bush safaris, where they go into the outback to do this.

Having lived this way of life for over thirty years now, I don't see it as a holiday; but then again, it is my way of life. I suppose I can understand how unique the situation is for someone who has never been 'bush'.

Clean air, sparkling stars in a crystal sky and time for songs and yarns around the camp fire. No pollution, traffic noise, lights, loud neighbours, lawn mowers, phones, faxes, parking problems or crowds.

Yes, I can see how the people from civilisation get blown away by an outback camp fire meal.

Opposite: Cold Mango Crab (recipe page 193).

November

Bullo Beef Burgers

~

Fresh Barra, Straight out of the River

~

Mum's Spicy Gingercake

~

Nora's Apple Sauce

~

Honey Baked Custard

~

Summer Plum Terrine

~

Orange Velvet Cream

~

Marlee's Iced Tea

~

Chicken with a Difference

~

Marinated Chilli-Lime Seafood

~

hile October has you wondering when the wet season will arrive, November leaves you in no doubt whatsoever. Sometimes November will give us a little rain, but mostly it sends heat, dry electric storms and violent dust storms that stretch across the entire landscape. The violence November can muster is sobering. It is the one month of the year that I'm glad to be away from home. In Darwin it's known as the crazy month; any strange behaviour in November is put down to people having 'gone troppo'.

There are some bonuses to November; all the staff have gone and a peaceful quiet descends over the house. It is so quiet at dawn, you can hear the birds singing. Gone is the loud exchange of the stockmen's friendly upstaging, rivalry and yarning. But Marlee and I still have a heavy work-load, so we start very early, well before the mid-morning heat makes it too hot to stay outside.

Light meals are back on the menu and we search for anything cold. Chewing ice becomes a pastime. Half-frozen fruit smoothies become whole meals. Even if your tastebuds crave something heavy, your digestive system doesn't and will throw it back up. Light meals are a must in November, to keep the stomach working normally.

Grilled steak, barra and chicken with lots of salad are served at lunch so the stomach has time to process the food before going to bed. Dinner is a very light meal, sometimes only fruit or an iced fruit smoothie with yoghurt and honey.

Some years when we are working into November on construction jobs we still have staff. I have seen some stubborn, 'I eat three big meals a day' men wolf down an enormous meal at dinner only to throw it up the next morning. They continue being sick as a dog all day, while watching Marlee work. Finally, they listen to me, and eat lightly at night.

There is nothing like a good grilled steak, but there are only so many cuts of meat on a steer that are suitable for grilling. We have to use up the rest of the meat, so a lot of the tougher cuts are made into mince.

Hamburgers are a popular meal on Bullo, served buffet-style, with all the ingredients to make a juicy meal on a big bun. This is my recipe.

Bullo Beef Burgers

1 kg finely minced good quality beef steak

3 tablespoons light or reduced-salt soy sauce

2 tablespoons grated ginger

3 tablespoons crushed garlic

2 tablespoons brown sugar

4 eggs, lightly beaten

½ cup chopped fresh parsley

4 onions, finely chopped

1 beef stock cube, crumbled

½ cup chicken stock

2 teaspoons mustard powder

Combine all the ingredients together in a large bowl; mix well. If mixture is too sloppy, add some cornflour or fresh breadcrumbs or some cooked rice. If too dry, add more chicken stock. The mixture should be slightly on the wet side.

Shape mixture with clean hands into balls, using about 2 rounded tablespoons of mixture per burger; flatten out to a patty shape. Don't have the burgers too thick, as they will burn on the outside before cooking on the inside, 2 cm is about right.

In a very heavy-based frying pan, brush the bottom with olive oil; place over a medium-high heat and, when the pan is hot, add some of the burgers. Cook until the bottom is sealed and the side is golden brown; turn over, reduce heat to medium-low and cook the burger through. Test by cutting a burger to reveal the centre.

Serve burgers with buns, toasted on the inside, sliced tomatoes, sliced beetroot, sliced onions, lettuce, chopped parsley, wholegrain mustard and tomato sauce.

MAKES 8

Chips are a favourite with this meal, either French fries or thick 'old style' chips. There are never chips left over; even total disasters cooked by the worst cooks are eaten. As long as it vaguely resembles a chip, it is eaten. Overcooked, undercooked, burnt to a cinder — it doesn't seem to matter.

I bake chips for myself and after just one taste the men all wanted 'my style' of chips. Instead of dropping the cut potatoes into oil, I use boiling water. I only let them boil for a minute and then spread them out in a greased shallow baking tray. I brush them very lightly with some oil, using a pastry brush, bake in a moderate oven (turning them once when golden brown) and finally sprinkle lightly with paprika, chopped parsley, and sometimes a very light sprinkle of parmesan. The men didn't want to go back to just ordinary chips.

I mentioned earlier what fresh barra straight out of the river tastes like — here is the recipe I used to cook it, 'plain and simple'.

Fresh Barra, Straight out of the River

6 fillets of barramundi, skinned
olive oil for cooking
2 cloves garlic, crushed
rind and juice of 1 lemon
½ cup chopped fresh parsley
freshly ground black pepper

Heat a large, very heavy-based frying pan over a medium–high heat; add 2 teaspoons of olive oil and cook garlic for 1 minute or so, stirring constantly. Scrape garlic from the pan.

Add fish fillets to pan, with 2 teaspoons oil per pan load of fish; add some lemon juice and sprinkle with some parsley. Cook until fillets are sealed underneath and fish is cooked half through. Turn over, sprinkle lightly with more parsley, lemon juice and black pepper. Cook until fish flakes easily with a fork.

Serve with rice or new potatoes, tossed in butter and parsley, and salad.

SERVES 6

I seem to be typing 'this is an American recipe' quite a lot, but the following recipe is only part American. The gingercake is actually one of my Mum's old recipes. If you want, you can just ice the cake and omit the apple sauce. The icing is mine and the apple sauce is American.

Mum's Spicy Gingercake

185 g unsalted butter

1 cup treacle

2 cups lightly packed dark brown sugar

4 cups plain flour

1 tablespoon baking powder

6 teaspoons ground ginger

1 teaspoon bicarbonate of soda

1 egg, lightly beaten

1¼ cups lukewarm milk

Place butter, treacle and brown sugar into a saucepan; stir over a low heat until sugar dissolves; allow to cool.

Sift flour, baking powder, ginger and bicarbonate of soda into a large mixing bowl. Add cooled sugar mixture, egg and warmed milk to the centre of the dry ingredients, make a well/hollow in the centre. Mix well until smoothly combined.

Pour mixture into 2 base-lined and greased deep round 20 cm cake tins.

Bake in a moderate oven/180°C, for 55 to 60 minutes, or until cooked when tested with a fine skewer. Allow cakes to cool slightly in tins before turning out onto a wire cooling rack to complete cooling.

Serve topped with Lemon-Lime Butter Icing (recipe page 78) or as a dessert, with Nora's Apple Sauce (see next recipe), whipped cream or with Honey Baked Custard (recipe page 211).

MAKES 2 CAKES; SERVES 16 – 24

Nora's Apple Sauce

Old Maryland recipe from America.

1 kg tart cooking apples
3 cups water
100 g light brown sugar
2 teaspoons ground cinnamon
½ teaspoon ground nutmeg
8 cloves
rind and juice of 2 lemons
50 g unsalted butter
2 tablespoon ground almonds

Cook sliced apples in a saucepan in water with sugar, cinnamon, nutmeg, cloves, lemon rind and juice. Bring to the boil and let boil for 3 minutes, uncovered. Reduce heat and simmer until liquid has evaporated.

Cool slightly, remove cloves, then whiz the mixture in a blender until a smooth sauce. Fold in butter and let melt through the sauce; stir in ground almonds.

Cut Spicy Gingercake into portions, spoon apple sauce over top with whipped cream and sliced fresh cherries or strawberries and serve.

SERVES 8 – 12

So many people buy commercial, ready-made custard. After my first dramatic failure at custard, I'm sure that if I lived in the city, I would've hot-footed it to the nearest supermarket and bought it by the litre.

But it was 1970 and I was out in the middle of nowhere so I tackled the job of making custard, without lumps. This was back in the days when I cooked for at least twenty people every day.

Being fairly practical, I couldn't see the sense in making custard daily, so I embarked on making enough for a few days; ten litres to be exact.

I mixed custard powder in a jug with some milk and sugar, then watched the ten litres of milk come to the boil. Following the instructions, I poured the dry mixture into the milk and stirred.

I was apparently a little too generous with the custard powder. The mixture turned to a solid lump and all ten litres became instant gluck. I frantically tried whisking but it just turned into lumpy gluck.

It couldn't be thrown away, so I set about changing it into something else.

I put it through a sieve (removing all the lumps), coloured the custard pink and added a few sultanas and vanilla.

This still wasn't enough, so next I spread the mixture out in a baking dish, sprinkled a 'crumble' mixture over the top, then covered everything heavily with pink coconut and baked it slowly in the oven. The result looked quite passable, so I cut it into squares and served it with cream. It was a great success.

However, I still needed to make normal custard and in large quantities. My troubles started when I added the custard mixture to the hot milk, so I decided to add it to cold milk instead. This method worked, and I never had lumpy custard again.

Making custard is also great for stress, because you have to stir until the milk comes to the boil. While you are standing stirring the custard you can take time to meditate, or bake the following.

Honey Baked Custard

2 large eggs
2 egg yolks
½ cup honey
2 cups milk
1 teaspoon vanilla essence

Preheat oven to 180°C.

Beat eggs, egg yolks and honey together in a mixing bowl. Heat milk until just below scalding point; gradually add to the egg mixture, beating constantly. Stir in the vanilla.

Pour the mixture into a baking dish and place in a roasting pan. Add enough hot water to reach halfway up the side of the baking dish to create a water bath. Bake for about 40 to 50 minutes, or until custard is firm.

Cool and refrigerate for at least 30 minutes before serving.

SERVES 8

Like our main courses, the desserts we eat in November are light, avoiding hot puddings or cakes with fillings that will melt in the heat.

Summer Plum Terrine

1.25 kg blood plums, stoned and sliced

1¼ cups caster sugar

2 teaspoons grated orange rind

1 cup fresh orange juice

¼ cup Grand Marnier

3 tablespoons gelatine

½ cup pine nuts

Line a deep rectangular 6-cup dish with clear plastic wrap.

Combine plums, sugar, orange rind, orange juice and Grand Marnier in large saucepan; stir over a medium heat, without boiling, until sugar is dissolved. Bring to the boil, reduce heat, cover and stew gently for about 15 minutes, or until plums are soft.

Sprinkle gelatine over ¼ cup water in a small heatproof bowl, mix well. Stand bowl in a pan of simmering water; stir gelatine mixture until dissolved. Quickly stir gelatine mixture into plum mixture. Transfer plum mixture to a bowl, cover and refrigerate until the mixture begins to set, then stir in the pine nuts.

Pour mixture into the prepared dish; cover and chill in the refrigerator for 3 hours or until set.

Turn plum terrine out onto a serving platter, remove plastic wrap. Serve with Orange Velvet Cream.

Orange Velvet Cream

6 teaspoons caster sugar

1 tablespoon water

2 egg yolks

2 teaspoons Grand Marnier

1 cup thickened cream

2 tablespoons grated orange rind

1 large orange, peeled, seeded, pith removed, and pureed in a blender

Combine sugar and water in small saucepan. Stir over a medium heat without boiling, until sugar is dissolved, then bring to the boil and remove from heat.

Beat egg yolks in the top of a double-boiler, over simmering water, with an electric mixer, until thick and creamy. Gradually beat in the hot sugar syrup; remove from heat. Cool to room temperature; stir in Grand Marnier.

Whip cream until thick; fold into the egg yolk mixture. Add orange rind and orange puree. Chill until ready to serve.

Serve with Summer Plum Terrine.

SERVES 6 – 8

Marlee's iced tea is so popular in the hot weather, she makes it in eighteen-litre batches. On working days it is alcohol-free, or stockmen would be staggering into the horns of a wild bull.

But for parties (with a little or a lot of alcohol) it is the most popular drink around. We've had a few funny incidents when Marlee didn't mention the tea was alcoholic. A few non-drinkers left parties very happy with the world, having no idea why. One woman, a very silent type, started talking after a few large glasses, and didn't stop. We could still hear her talking and laughing as the car drove away.

Her husband remarked many times during the night he had never seen her so talkative in all their married life.

Seeing they were both very much teetotallers, we decided to let the subject of alcohol in the tea slip. They went away extremely happy with the world in general.

Marlee's Iced Tea

4 litres weak tea
6 oranges
6 lemons
2 limes
honey to taste
sugar to taste
2 cups dark rum or more
1 cup orange brandy or more,
depending on taste

Make tea and leave to cool, then chill, covered, in the refrigerator.

Thinly slice oranges, lemons and limes; remove seeds but do not peel the fruit. Add sliced citrus fruit to tea. Add honey and sugar to taste, not too sweet though, as orange brandy is still to come.

At this stage, you have a nice iced tea, after you let it chill and settle for a few hours.

However, if you want a party punch, stir in the rum and orange brandy. How much depends on you, but Marlee's guide is 2 cups of rum and 1 cup of brandy. But it's all up to personal taste! Serve in tall glasses.

SERVES 16 – 20 APPROXIMATELY

By now the days are so hot that all food is kept in the fridge or chiller. Butter and cream turn to grease puddles in minutes and even butter biscuits will go rancid if not refrigerated.

When I am putting all food in sight in the chiller, I think of my first visit to Maryland. We arrived in winter – it was twenty degrees below on the Fahrenheit scale – and most of the food was kept on a screened porch.

It took me weeks to get used to taking meat out of the kitchen and just leaving it on a shelf on a screened porch. It just didn't seem right, having just flown in from northern Australia and one-hundred-and-ten degrees Fahrenheit! Meat left anywhere other than the chiller on Bullo would have been carried away by meat ants attacked by flies or gone off.

But of course, a porch at minus twenty was much colder than the fridge in the kitchen. Sometimes I would make the mistake of putting orange juice and milk out there at night, only to find them both frozen solid the next morning. This memory was long forgotten until a few years ago when I visited Austria and Franz's mother put the meat out on the balcony.

Below is an American recipe going back to 1824, for a baked chicken pudding, similar to Toad in the Hole. It is something a little different and just perfect for those hot November evenings.

Chicken with a Difference

2 x 1.5 kg chickens
1 teaspoon salt
½ teaspoon peppercorns
about a handful of celery tops
1 onion, sliced
¼ cup chopped fresh parsley
1 teaspoon fresh thyme
5 large eggs
2 cups milk
2 cups plain flour
60 g (¼ cup) butter, melted
extra ½ teaspoon salt

Cut chickens into serving pieces and remove skin where possible. Place chicken pieces in a large heavy-based pan or boiler.

Add salt, peppercorns, celery tops, onion, parsley and thyme to pan. Cover chicken with boiling water, and simmer, covered, until chicken is almost tender (not fully cooked), about 30–45 minutes.

Remove the best chicken pieces from the pan leaving the backbones, necks and wings in the pan. Simmer the stock, uncovered, until it is rich and reduced in volume. Strain stock and set aside.

Arrange chicken pieces in a single layer in a baking dish. Add ½ cup of the chicken stock.

Sift flour and salt into a mixing bowl. Make a well (hollow) in the centre. In a second bowl, beat eggs until very light. Add eggs, milk and melted butter to the flour mixture and mix to a smooth batter, beating well with a wooden spoon.

Pour this over the chicken and bake in a hot oven/ 200°C until pudding is set and a nice golden brown, 20 to 30 minutes.

Make a gravy out of the chicken stock and serve very hot with the chicken pudding. Serve with potatoes and other favourite vegetables.

SERVES 8

Flying around the world and seeing different countries, foods and customs is fun, but there is a time when I get homesick and need to get back to familiar things. Things like putting food in the chiller and temperatures going above zero once in a while. Familiar things make you relax and feel that you belong.

On one overseas trip, I travelled for over two months and was in countries where very little English was spoken. I felt quite alone and isolated, despite the people being friendly and helpful, and I anxiously stepped on board my Qantas plane, heading for home.

I was greeted by the friendly Australian voice of the air hostess.

'Welcome aboard.'

'Oh, it's so good to be home!' I replied.

The air hostess laughed and said that I was actually a long way from home in Frankfurt, Germany.

What she didn't realise was that, for me, a Qantas plane is a little bit of Australia, flying around the world. The moment I stepped on board, I felt at home. Everything was familiar.

Even though it was hot when I eventually arrived back at Bullo, it didn't matter. I was home and everything was familiar once again.

Opposite: Marble Cheesecake (recipe page 225) and My Favourite 'Normal' Cheesecake (recipe page 227). Following page: Marinated Chilli-Lime Seafood (recipe page 217).

The following recipe is really delicious and makes a nice change from the usual way we serve barramundi.

Marinated Chilli-Lime Seafood

Marinade:

½ cup canola or peanut oil

2 teaspoons cumin seeds, crushed

2 teaspoons coriander seeds, crushed

3 cloves garlic, crushed

2 small fresh red chillies, finely chopped

1½ teaspoons grated lime rind

1 teaspoon grated orange rind

⅓ cup lime juice

⅓ cup orange juice

½ cup red wine vinegar

2 teaspoons sugar

1 teaspoon paprika

Seafood:

4 medium barramundi fillets or large whiting fillets, skinned

500 g medium green prawns

2 eggs, lightly beaten

2 tablespoons plain flour

1 teaspoon celery salt

canola or peanut oil for frying

freshly cooked rice for serving

chopped fresh parsley and sliced spring onions/shallots for garnish

To make Marinade: Heat oil in a pan, add seeds, garlic and chillies and cook, stirring, until fragrant. Add the remaining marinade ingredients; simmer, uncovered, for 2 minutes. Cool marinade until cold.

Remove any bones from the fish fillets; cut fish into strips 1 cm wide. Shell and devein prawns, leaving the tail segment attached.

Place fish and prawns in a bowl. Add marinade and mix gently to coat. Cover and marinate in the refrigerator, from 3 to 6 hours. Drain well and reserve marinade.

Combine eggs, flour and celery salt in a mixing bowl; beat until smooth. Add fish and prawns; mix gently to coat the fish and prawns evenly.

In a heavy-based frying pan, fry the fish and prawns in 5 mm hot oil, over a medium–high heat, a few at a time, until golden brown. Drain well on paper towels. Keep hot. Continue until all fish is cooked.

Serve fish hot on freshly cooked rice, sprinkled with chopped parsley and spring onions. Heat reserved marinade and pour over the seafood and rice. Serve with salad.

SERVES 4 – 6

In November, the dogs are back to leaning on the door of the air-conditioned office, howling to get in. In the early days, when there was no airconditioning, we had to 'sweat' it out together in the heat. Now we race each other to get into the cool air, first thing each morning.

I catch up on accounts, not done for months during the mustering season, open mail, make the phone calls put off for months and write. If I'm working on a book and there is a manuscript delivery date close at hand, I start work in November. Otherwise, writing starts later in January and February. Meanwhile, there is plenty of office work and correspondence to fill every day.

At the end of the day, when the sun surrenders its possessive hold over the day, we come out to play and I run down the airstrip. The weather is such in November that I can start out on a two kilometre run with the weather still hot and the sky clear, but when I turn at the end of the strip to come home, the sky to the north-east has turned black and menacing.

A low black mass of cloud will be bearing down on the valley at an amazing speed, throwing bolts of lightning in all directions as it propels itself forward, cracking and hurling thunder booms so loud and low that the ground vibrates.

The race is on to get back indoors before the homestead disappears, consumed by the storm, or the dogs and I are caught in the fury or hit by a lightning bolt. Sometimes we make it in the door just ahead of the downpour, sometimes we don't.

One way or the other I usually sit and watch the first storm of the season. This has developed into a tradition on Bullo – Charlie again. Everyone had to stop work (something he did at the beginning of the day!) and drink to celebrate the first rain of the season.

If it happens in November, we can be hopeful of a good wet. But these storms are almost always violent; fast, sudden, heavy downpours, gone after too little rain and leaving too much damage. But it is rain and in whatever form we must have it.

So we will pause to drink to the new rainy season, even if it is only with a glass of water.

December

Creamy Fresh Fruit Fluff

~

Coconut Thins

~

Marble Cheesecake

~

My Favourite 'Normal' Cheesecake

~

Egg Nog

~

Eggs Benedict

~

My Mum's Crunchy Stuffing

~

Baked Sweet Potato, Maryland-Style

~

Pavlova with Marlee's Special Filling

~

The morning after the first storm of the season everything and everyone is silent. Grass struggles to stand. It is plastered flat to the ground, encased in dried mud.

The birds are busy drying their wings so they can fly out to find their morning meal before the heat of the day makes this an unpleasant task.

The only movement comes from hordes of mosquitoes, looking for the last bite before sunlight sends them scurrying into some dark, dank refuge. The first call of the day from a lone bird warns them they have dallied too long.

Dawn comes with this one lone call; soon answered by another, then another, and the valley comes alive with the song of thousands. The busy month of December has to somehow fit in between the storms, no matter how violent or how regular they are. We wait for enough rain to soak the ground and then the ploughing starts.

A trip to Darwin for Christmas shopping has to be fitted into a schedule that is full of people dropping by 'the last time' before the wet.

Christmas party invitations arrive daily from Darwin, Katherine, Kununurra, Sydney and Melbourne. To attend would take us all month and we would need a Concorde to get around. We are mostly too busy to attend all but a few, and only then if the weather is kind and we can fly.

Ploughing usually starts around the second half of December. The first half is quickly gobbled up by shopping for Christmas presents, shopping for food, attending a few Christmas parties in Darwin, doing the Christmas mail and bringing in the 'wet' supplies by truck. The phone slows down to one call an hour, instead of ringing off the hook as it does for the rest of the year.

We do a last trip around the lower paddocks checking fences and animals. This is now done on a four-wheeler bike, making the job a breeze. The girls did it back when they were young, but it was not an easy job then. They had to put all the fencing material onto a pack mule and ride around the fences on a horse. There was alway great preparation for the 'boundary rides'. Beef jerky was made ahead of time.

On special occasions, when checking fences close to the homestead, they were allowed to camp out for the night. There was always great discussion over the menu, but they usually settled on steak cooked on a shovel over their camp fire for lunch, followed by a barra caught in the river and cooked on the river bank for dinner.

Twenty-five years ago, there were no crocs around the homestead or further up into the gorge area. We would often spend all day picnicking beside the river, while the children and the dogs would jump in the river with not a croc in sight.

Today I wouldn't put a toe in any part of the Bullo River. There are so many crocs now, they come out of the river into the paddocks and take our cattle. The spot where we used to picnic at the end of the airstrip is now the territory of a three-metre croc. We never go fishing or fencing without a shotgun at our side. We had one occasion where a croc bit a big barra in half while it was still on the hook, being hauled ashore!

As the storms increase, we find ourselves doing more inside jobs and finally have the opportunity to watch some TV. By this time though, the programs are mostly repeats and forty-year-old movies.

While Marlee does saddle and bridle repairs, I amuse myself by telling her who the actors are and if they are still alive. This drives her up the wall but keeps me amused, then the phone rings and she is left in peace.

In between ploughing, we go round to the breeding paddocks, looking at the new calves and foals. This is one of the great pleasures of the year – seeing these beautiful babies makes you feel all the work was worthwhile.

When it rains for days on end and we have caught up on the 'inside' jobs, we can indulge ourselves and cook something totally naughty, but totally delicious. The cold desserts are back in great demand. The following are quick, easy and tasty.

Creamy Fresh Fruit Fluff

500 g peaches, stoned, peeled and sliced

250 g nectarines, stoned, peeled and sliced

250 g apricots, stoned, peeled and sliced

¼ cup caster sugar

2 tablespoons honey

1 tablespoon lemon juice

1 teaspoon ground nutmeg

2 tablespoons arrowroot

2 tablespoons water

½ cup light sour cream

whipped cream, extra sliced fruit, 4 tablespoons Grand Marnier and ½ teaspoon caster sugar for serving

Mix in a food processor the peaches, nectarines, apricots, sugar, honey, lemon juice and nutmeg, until smooth; pour into a saucepan.

Blend arrowroot smoothly with water; stir into fruit mixture. Place over a medium heat, stirring constantly, until mixture boils and thickens. Cool.

Stir sour cream into fruit mixture. Pour into 8 dessert glasses, about ½-cup capacity, and refrigerate for several hours until firm.

Serve with Coconut Thins (see recipe below), whipped cream and sliced fresh peaches, nectarines and apricots, sprinkled with a mixture of 4 tablespoons Grand Marnier and ½ teaspoon caster sugar.

Serves 8

Coconut Thins

30 g unsalted butter

1½ tablespoons caster sugar

1½ tablespoons honey

1 teaspoon lemon juice

1 tablespoon plain flour

2 tablespoons desiccated coconut

Beat butter and sugar in a small mixing bowl until light and creamy. Add honey and lemon juice and beat until fluffy. Fold in flour and coconut.

Place 1 level teaspoon of mixture, 5 cm apart, on a greased baking tray. Bake in a moderately slow oven/160°C, for 15 minutes or until golden brown.

Allow to stand on baking tray for 1 minute until firm then carefully transfer to a wire cooling rack to cool.

Marble Cheesecake made by Marlee is another favourite. In December she makes up a big batch for friends dropping by. This recipe was given to me by my sister-in-law Frances. I asked her if she could remember how she came by it, but she couldn't.

One day I was going through one of Mum's old recipe books and there it was — a cutting from one of the weekly magazines, pasted in her book. It seems it won first prize in a cooking competition held by the magazine. Mrs J Matinovich of Brisbane won the first prize with this recipe. I have no idea how old the clipping is, but it has to be twenty-five years at least.

So Mrs Matinovich of Brisbane, if you are out there, your marble cheesecake went from Brisbane to Sydney, to Mum, to Fran, finally travelling to me to Bullo River in the Northern Territory. At Bullo it was served to the American Ambassador and his wife.

The recipe was quickly requested and it then travelled to Canberra where it became part of the Embassy menu. I received a photo of fifty marble cheesecakes sitting on a table waiting to be served at a formal function.

From Canberra it went back to California, where its reputation spread. It is still cooking up a storm, as it is back on Bullo.

Marble Cheesecake

125 g dark cooking chocolate
150 g unsalted butter
125 g cream cheese
1 cup caster sugar
3 large eggs
½ cup, plus 1 tablespoon, plain flour
1 teaspoon vanilla essence
¼ teaspoon baking powder
½ cup coarsely chopped walnuts
¼ teaspoon almond essence

Melt the chocolate and 100 g butter in a heatproof bowl over a pan of simmering hot water, stirring occasionally. Cool.

Cream remaining butter with cream cheese. Gradually add ¼ cup sugar, beating until light and fluffy. Add 1 egg and beat well. Stir in 1 tablespoon flour and ½ teaspoon vanilla. Set aside.

Beat remaining eggs and remaining sugar until thick and light. Sift remaining flour and baking powder into egg mixture, fold in gently. Add the cooled chocolate mixture, walnuts, almond essence and remaining vanilla. Stir gently until combined.

Measure 1 cup of chocolate mixture and set aside. Spread remaining chocolate mixture into a lined and greased 23 cm square cake tin. Top with cream cheese mixture, then drop spoonfuls of reserved chocolate mixture on top. Swirl a knife through the mixture to make a marble pattern.

Bake in a moderate oven/180°C, for 40-45 minutes. Place cheesecake on a wire cooling rack and allow to cool in tin. Cut into squares; cover and allow to set in refrigerator. This cheesecake freezes well, but never lasts that long.

SERVES 9 – 12

This recipe has always been Marlee's famous cheesecake. When I brought the recipe back to Bullo, it sat in the recipe bookcase for a while until Marlee made it. Then it was hers for evermore.

My claim to fame in the cheesecake arena happened about twenty years earlier. I made my first cheesecake in Sydney for a dinner party I had for Susan.

As usual, with Charlie around, I was in a state of perpetual panic. The cheesecake turned out okay, but I made a bit of a mess cutting the layers and while arguing with Charlie, I dropped it onto the serving platter.

First-time recipes for dinner parties and Charlie were not a good mix, but I patched it together as best I could.

A friend of Susan's arrived with what could only be described as the perfect cheesecake and plonked it down next to my crumbled mess. Naturally, everyone went for the beautifully decorated cheesecake, including me. It looked utterly irresistible. But it was … yuck! It had no taste at all and was like eating glug, you needed glasses of water to get it down. Cheesecake was abandoned everywhere, in non-conspicuous places, with only one spoonful missing.

With only my patched-up cheesecake left, it was approached with great scepticism. The other one looked fabulous and tasted like hell, mine looked like hell, but tasted fabulous. It disappeared in seconds.

My Favourite 'Normal' Cheesecake

375 g light cream cheese
¾ cup caster sugar
4 large eggs
6 teaspoons gelatine
2 tablespoons cold water
1 tablespoon lemon juice
300 ml cream
icing sugar for decoration
1 x 20 cm sponge cake
½ teaspoon ground cinnamon
½ teaspoon ground nutmeg
grated rind of 1 lemon

Beat together cream cheese and sugar in bowl with an electric mixer for 5 minutes. Add eggs one at a time, beating well after each addition.

Soak gelatine in cold water in a small heatproof bowl. Add lemon juice and place in a hot-water bath, stirring occasionally, until dissolved.

Add gelatine mixture to cream cheese mixture, mix well. Whip cream until stiff; fold into cream cheese mixture.

Line a 20 cm springform cake tin with clear plastic wrap, allowing a generous amount of wrap to fold over the top of the cheesecake when finished.

Slice sponge cake into 3 horizontal layers. Use top and bottom layers only; use the middle layer for a trifle. Place the bottom layer in the bottom of the prepared tin, on top of the clear plastic wrap.

Sprinkle the sponge with half the ground cinnamon, ground nutmeg and grated lemon rind; spoon in the cheese mixture; sprinkle with remaining cinnamon, nutmeg and the lemon rind. Place the top layer of sponge on top; sprinkle generously with icing sugar, covering the top of the cake completely.

Carefully tie the plastic wrap across the top of the cake to keep everything in place. Refrigerate for several hours or overnight until firm.

Serve chilled.

SERVES 8 – 12

Marlee and I head for Darwin the first clear, cloudless morning we get. Franz has the tractor parked at the gate into the paddock with the motor running, waiting impatiently for the sun and morning breeze to dry the ground so he can start ploughing. We race around Darwin in the rain and the heat and think of presents for everyone. We buy Christmas cards with great intentions of sending them out, but usually take them home to Bullo to sit for another year.

All the presents that we buy have to fit in the plane with all the food and us. If one of us decides on a large present, the arrangements need to be made months ahead so the gift can be trucked to Katherine, then picked up with the wet supplies by our truck at the beginning of December.

Large presents bought in late December arrive on Bullo in late April, after the road is open.

A plane packed to capacity arrives back to a changed landscape. Wide sweeps of tilled brown earth greet us, in between flowing fields of long, green grass. Hawks are slowly circling, behind the plough, waiting for it to turn up easy pickings for them.

As the discs disturb a nest of baby king browns, the watching birds dive rapidly, in perfect formation, peeling off one by one to sweep in for the kill. Before the tractor has gone twenty metres, all evidence of the baby snakes has gone.

We circle the field and waggle the wings, Franz waves back. New calves and foals bolt in terror as they watch the strange, noisy thing in the sky approaching. Their mothers look up casually at the plane, lower their heads and go on eating. The babies, taking lead from their mothers, settle down. It is so good to see the green paddocks stretching into the distant horizon, so restful on the eyes after months of brown and dust.

The plane comes to a halt under the watchful eyes of all the animals. Everything is unloaded; Christmas presents are hidden and the food is stacked in the chiller and freezer. The Christmas CDs are taken out of the cupboard, dusted off, and played daily. The countdown to Christmas begins and the cooking and preparation for Christmas starts.

Plum pudding and Christmas cake are first on the agenda. I busy myself with this task, while Marlee drives the other tractor to help Franz.

The next preparation is Egg Nog – this is a very big part of Christmas on Bullo. I make it two days ahead and keep it freezing cold.

Egg Nog

This recipe was given to me thirty-four years ago, by a Spanish friend in Manila, the Philippines. It's a very potent Christmas drink, and it only comes once a year, so this recipe is OK as long as you are not driving. 'Just as well' you will say after reading the following.

The whole recipe is prepared with an electric mixer. You will need to go into training if you are old-fashioned and want to mix it by hand. In which case, you should start six weeks ahead and go into training in early November! If you are like me and prefer the modern machines, born out of years of mixing with a wooden spoon when we had no electricity on the station, take a large electric mixer and do the following:

You will need:

12 large free-range eggs, separated

pinch of salt

2 tablespoons caster sugar

4 cups rum

2 cups good quality brandy

1 cup good Scotch whisky

1 litre full cream milk, chilled

600 ml cream, chilled

freshly grated nutmeg for decoration

We are making a winter drink in the summer, so make sure the eggs are really fresh before mixing. Also put the mixing bowl in the refrigerator for an hour or so before starting.

Whisk egg whites and salt in the cleanly polished, chilled bowl of an electric mixer, until very stiff. Put into another bowl, cover and refrigerator.

Put into the same mixing bowl, (no need to wash anything), the egg yolks and sugar; beat well. Slowly add the rum, brandy and whisky, beating constantly until combined (for variations see end of recipe).

Mix well and put in the freezer, in a suitable container, for a few hours, or in the refrigerator overnight, if you are organised and have the time.

In a large punch bowl, put the egg yolk and liquor mixture; add the milk and mix well. Whip the cream until thick.

Fold the whipped cream and whisked egg whites into the egg yolk mixture. Cover the top of the egg nog with freshly grated nutmeg.

Put in the refrigerator for 4 hours, then keep refrigerated until ready to serve.

If you don't use it all (not very likely), you can freeze what is left over and make alcoholic ice cream for New Year!

SERVES 24 APPROXIMATELY

Variations

Now this is a 'good old days' recipe and after a 'good day' of the above, you usually woke up in time for New Year, so, seeing we are far more health-conscious in the nineties, the following are variations on the theme.

3 cups rum		2 cups rum		you can reduce
1½ cups brandy	or	1 cup brandy	or	again to very
¾ cup whisky		½ cup whisky		little alcohol

It is nearly Christmas Day and the storms are coming more frequently. Ploughing slows down almost to a half, as the ground gets too wet to work, but at least Franz can stop for Christmas and get the Christmas tree.

This was another exciting adventure for the girls when they were young. They set out early in the morning and spent most of the day in search of the right Christmas tree. They chopped it down and dragged the chosen tree back home behind a sometimes not so willing horse. We had lots of leafless Christmas trees over the years when the horse took fright and exception to the towing arrangements and just bolted for home at full speed. But the girls had loads of fun. These days it is a quick, short trip in the Toyota with a chainsaw to do the work.

On Christmas Eve, Franz and Marlee return with a tree. It is given pride of place in the centre of the living room, ready for decorating. We decorate the tree at sunset, then arrange all the presents under it, ready for Christmas morning.

Gone are the days of crawling around in the dark at 3.00 am, putting out the girls' presents from Santa. It is all quite civilised now.

We usually eat ham and mustard sandwiches, fruit cake and drink egg nog while decorating the tree. On his first year at Bullo Franz was horrified that we didn't eat dinner. After eating everything on the plates, he went on to consume bacon, eggs and toast followed with a large salad. So now Marlee prepares a big dinner on Christmas Eve.

The first thing on the menu on Christmas morning is opening the presents. No matter how old Marlee gets, the presents under the Christmas tree still take top priority.

Franz is even worse, wanting to open the presents on Christmas Eve! He keeps saying, 'It's a tradition in Austria to open the presents on Christmas Eve.'

I keep saying, 'Well, it's not on Bullo.'

So they are both ready very early on Christmas morning. Franz even puts off breakfast to open his presents, and that is quite something for Franz.

We sip egg nog while opening the presents then head straight for the kitchen to make a late breakfast. Breakfast is a big meal because we don't eat Christmas dinner until late in the day when the weather cools. So breakfast is really brunch. We start with Eggs Benedict.

Eggs Benedict

Served by Marlee for Christmas breakfast.

2 teaspoons butter

4 slices cooked ham

2 English muffins, split, or any favourite bread

extra butter for muffins

4 eggs

Hollandaise Sauce:

90 g butter

2 tablespoons strained lemon juice

2 egg yolks

2 teaspoons water

pinch of salt

freshly ground white pepper

Melt butter in a non-stick frying pan and cook ham until golden brown on each side. Keep warm.

Toast muffins and spread with butter; arrange on individual serving plates and top with ham; keep warm.

Poach eggs in simmering water, in a frying pan, with ½ teaspoon salt and 1 tablespoon cider vinegar (or poach in an egg poacher). Carefully slide each egg from a saucer into the water and cook, uncovered, until eggs are done as you like them. Should take about 4 minutes.

Remove eggs with an eggslice and drain thoroughly before placing on the ham and muffins.

To make Hollandaise Sauce: Have butter at room temperature, cut into small pieces, the size of a teaspoon.

Put one knob/piece of butter, lemon juice, egg yolks and water into the top of a double-boiler. Beat with a balloon-whisk until well combined. Then place over simmering water, add salt and pepper and beat until mixture thickens to form a smooth cream.

Remove from heat; add remaining butter, one piece at a time, and beat well until absorbed into sauce.

Spoon the sauce over the eggs, ham and muffins.

Serve accompanied with orange juice, laced with champagne, with sliced strawberries and mint leaves floating on top.

SERVES 4

*Opposite: Christmas Breakfast at Bullo. Egg Nog (recipe page 229) and Eggs Benedict (recipe this page).
Following pages: Sara and Marlee enjoying Marlee's Iced Tea (recipe page 214).*

While Marlee and I recover from this amazing dish, Franz is looking for more food. So it is my turn and I make a big batch of my Mum's pancakes.

Franz eats them with everything. He can eat any quantity of food and never put on weight. Marlee and I watch with envy as Franz finishes all the food and looks for more! We retire to bed and sleep through the heat of the day in blessed air-conditioned comfort.

Early afternoon and it's time for the turkey to go in the oven. Cooking turkey brings back so many memories, especially memories of the turkeys on the station in 1970.

Being a city girl, I had never seen a live turkey until I got to Bullo. I took a dislike to the gobbler, he was a super chauvinist pig! He was very mean to the other turkeys, so I took to him with the broom whenever I saw this behaviour. When Charlie told one of the men to catch him for Christmas dinner, it was fine by me.

The stockman chased him around the pen, then took a flying leap and grabbed the bird by the tail. The turkey let out a frightful noise and leaped in the air leaving his tail behind in the stockman's hand, as he went over the fence and down the flat. A younger turkey was caught and cooked.

The bare-bottomed turkey came slinking back to the turkey run a changed bird – he was meek and mild and nice. But the others took their revenge, acted as he did before he lost his feathers and made his life hell. His tail grew back and so did all his nasty, arrogant character. Once again, he ruled the roost.

Here is a priceless gem from an old American cookbook published 1890 in Washington, DC.

TO PREPARE A TURKEY FOR CHRISTMAS DINNER

The turkey should be cooped up and fed some time before Christmas. Then, three days before it is slaughtered, it should have an English walnut forced down its throat three times a day, along with a glass of sherry, only once a day. The meat will be deliciously tender, and have a fine nutty flavour.

All I can deduce from these amazing instructions is that people had a lot of time on their hands in 1890 and the turkeys were a lot tamer than the ones I met on Bullo.

Opposite: Pavlova with Marlee's Special Filling (recipe page 236).

Waiting till evening makes for a much more enjoyable meal, but we are very hungry by the end of the day. We have the traditional turkey, ham and all the trimmings.

I won't go into all the preparation, we all know it so well and have our own special recipes and ways to cook the turkey.

But there are two recipes that I would like to share with you. These are my Mum's crunchy stuffing and an old Maryland recipe for baked sweet potatoes that I brought back with me from America.

My Mum's Crunchy Stuffing

6 slices multi-grain bread, crumbled into small pieces

1 cup day-old or stale breadcrumbs

2 onions, finely chopped

6 mushrooms, finely chopped

1 clove garlic, crushed

4 tomatoes, chopped

1 cup chopped fresh parsley

1 teaspoon chopped fresh chives

1 teaspoon chopped fresh basil

½ cup cranberry sauce

⅓ cup chopped almonds

⅓ cup chopped walnuts

1 chicken stock cube, crumbled

pinch of dried mixed herbs

½ cup light or reduced-salt soy sauce

2 cups beer

chicken stock to mix

salt and freshly ground black pepper

Combine all the ingredients and mix well. Season to taste with salt and pepper. Make the stuffing fairly wet, using more chicken stock if necessary.

Use some of the stuffing to stuff the turkey and spread the rest in a greased, shallow baking dish, about 1.5 cm thick.

For a topping, combine together in a bowl:

1 cup fresh breadcrumbs

1 cup chopped fresh parsley

30 g butter, melted

Mix the butter into the mixture and sprinkle over the stuffing in the baking dish.

Bake in a moderate oven/180°C, for 30 minutes or until golden brown and crunchy on top.

If you bake it in a nice ovenproof serving dish, it can go straight to the table for serving as is.

We like to have the following baked sweet potato recipe, along with our normal baked potatoes.

Baked Sweet Potato, Maryland-Style

1 kg even-sized orange sweet potatoes/kumara

Stuffing:

½ cup light brown sugar

⅓ cup maple syrup

¼ cup lemon juice

2 teaspoons grated lemon rind

20 g (2 tablespoons) butter, melted

1 teaspoon French mustard

1 teaspoon grated fresh ginger

¼ cup Grand Marnier

salt and fresh ground black pepper

Topping:

½ cup fresh breadcrumbs

½ cup chopped fresh parsley

10 g (2 teaspoons) melted butter

Wash and peel the sweet potatoes; cut in half lengthwise. Bake in a hot oven/200°C, on a baking tray until about half cooked, about 20 minutes. Remove from oven and let cool until easy to handle.

Scoop out as much of the inside of each sweet potato as possible, into a mixing bowl, leaving a 5 mm shell on the potato halves.

To make Stuffing: Combine the sweet potato in the bowl with all the stuffing ingredients and salt and pepper to taste; mix well. Fill the sweet potato shells with the sweet potato mixture.

To make Topping: Mix breadcrumbs with parsley and melted butter.

Sprinkle topping evenly over the stuffed sweet potatoes. Bake in a moderate oven/180°C, until potatoes are cooked and tops nicely golden brown, about 20 minutes. If tops do not brown and potatoes are cooked, put under the grill for a few minutes.

Serve with Christmas turkey.

SERVES 6 – 8

While all this is cooking, I prepare the rest of the vegetables. The dining table is groaning beneath all of the food: roast turkey with stuffing and gravy, baked potatoes, sweet potatoes, broccoli with hollandaise sauce, and carrots. We also have ham baked with cloves and a honey and brown sugar coating, lots of cranberry sauce and hot crunchy bread rolls.

Whew, it's just as well Christmas is only once a year!

The sun is just setting and we drink champagne, mango and strawberry iced smoothies in Charlie's crystal goblets. Then we settle down to the wonderful Christmas feast on the table before us.

It is cool outside under a dull sky. After a few hours' rest from food we enjoy Marlee's Pavlova, the cool change and a hot coffee.

Pavlova with Marlee's Special Filling

3 egg whites
pinch of salt
¾ cup caster sugar
¼ cup white sugar
1 tablespoon cornflour
1 teaspoon lemon juice

Whisk egg whites with salt in a clean polished mixing bowl, with an electric mixer, until soft peaks form. Add caster sugar gradually, beating constantly. Make sure sugar is completely dissolved after each addition, before adding the next amount.

(Because we are in such heat, we chill the bowl and the eggs until we need to use them, and also pick a nice clear, dry sunny day, with no humidity, as this can affect the sugar.)

Mix together white sugar and cornflour; lightly fold into meringue mixture with lemon juice.

Line a baking tray with baking paper or greaseproof paper. Draw a 23 cm circle on the paper and dust lightly with cornflour.

Spread a 1.5 cm layer of the meringue mixture to fit the circle. Then, around the edge of the circle, on top

Marlee's Special Filling:

4 bananas

300 ml thickened cream

250 g cream cheese

6 passionfruit, 4 for filling, 2 for decoration

extra cream, whipped, for decoration

4 kiwifruit, peeled and sliced

1 punnet strawberries, sliced

any other fruit to your liking, although the above seems to be a 'spot-on' combination

of the meringue, build up the meringue by piping the rest of the meringue in swirls. You should end up with a pie-shaped shell.

Bake in a very slow oven/120°C, for 1½ to 2 hours. The meringue is cooked when it feels dry and crisp. Do not remove from the oven, but turn off the heat; leave the door ajar and let the pavlova cool in the oven. Remove after an hour or so.

To make Marlee's Special Filling: Puree two of the bananas, whip the cream and cream cheese together and fold banana puree into the cream mixture. Add passionfruit pulp from 4 passionfruit.

Fill the inside of the shell with this filling.

Decorate the top of the meringue with piped whipped cream around the edge. Cover the filling with remaining passionfruit pulp. Place remaining sliced bananas, sprinkled with lemon juice, around edge of filling. Decorate with sliced kiwifruit and strawberries. Serve immediately.

SERVES 12

We tell Franz about Christmas past and he tells us about Christmas in Austria. Thinking back, I have spent Christmas in many different places: Sydney, Hong Kong, Philippines, Bullo River and America. We lived in New York for six months, but missed out on having Christmas in New York by a few weeks. Danielle was due on December 25 so we went back to Maryland for the birth. But the house we lived in on the West Side was supposed to be where *'twas the Night Before Christmas* was written. The children spent the whole six months asking, 'Was it here, did he write it here?'

One big family Christmas was spent in Bargara with Mum and Susan, Ralph and Tod and Fran. One was at sea, in the comfort of a luxury cruise ship and another at sea in ultimate discomfort on one of Charlie's nightmare sailing trips, where everything that could go wrong, did.

But Bullo is the place I like best to spend Christmas.

On Boxing Day Marlee and Franz go back to ploughing. The dogs and I retire to the cool of the office and to the piles of work awaiting me. They curl around the base of my chair, winding their legs in and out of the roller caster, making it impossible for me to move the chair until they decide to stand.

Another year is drawing to a close, another terrible storm is building, the signs are everywhere. Amazing cloud sculptures crowd the sky, spectacular colour combinations appear out of nowhere and then change swiftly.

The heat is stifling and sweat pours out of you, even when you are not moving.

The sunset warns that the storm is very near. Too brilliant a display of colour, too high a temperature and a deafening silence so eerie it makes the hair on the back of your neck stand on end. As night falls, silent lightning flashes endlessly across the sky.

After a day of intense heat the storm arrives meekly in the dark of night. Soft rain gradually increases to a consistent downpour and the temperature drops to a pleasant 29°C. The rain lasts all night, cancelling any hope of work. It takes two days for the paddocks to dry.

Once again it is New Year's Eve, we are racing to finish planting and the next storm is sitting patiently on the horizon.

I walk into the kitchen early and find a note from Marlee saying they started at midnight, hoping to finish before this storm hits. I watch the weather report on the morning news. A monster front is approaching the northern part of Australia and is not that far away.

There will be no midnight supper in the field this year.

At 9.00 pm the door bursts open and the dogs tumble into the kitchen, yapping and yowling an enthusiastic welcome. Marlee and Franz are not far behind.

The crop is planted! The storm is still sitting on the distant horizon, flashing continuous lightning, but not a sound of thunder is reaching us.

Marlee and Franz shower and change into clean clothes. Marlee bounds into the kitchen fresh and bright, 'What's to eat, Mum? We're starved!'

It has toppled empires
and defeated the greatest armies.

It can put you on top of the world
or in the depths of despair.

It can inspire you to fight forever
or make you too weak to lift a finger.

It can cause disease
and it can cure disease.

It can alter your mind
and it has the power to destroy humanity.

What can it be?

Power?
Money?
Sex?
Sin?
Greed?
Pestilence?
Plague?
Disease?

No, it's none of the above.

It's food.

Index